HAPPY CLOUD MEDIA LLC PRESENTS:

EXPLOITATION NATION

MR. BRUNELLE EXPLAINS IT ALL!	2
DOWN THE RABBIT HOLE	3
GOODBYE CARMINE	8
STOP READING, STOP BREATHING	16
TOP 100 MOST BANNED AND CHALLENGED BOOKS: 2010-2019	19
A FEW MINUTES WITH ALEX COX	22
ARE WE THERE YET? CRONENBERG'S CRASH	28
DEAR SANTA, THIS YEAR, I'D LIKE YOU TO GO AWAY	36
THE MOTION PICTURE PRODUCTION CODE	40
LINNEA QUIGLEY'S CHRISTMAS STALKING	44
TRANSPORTER 2 (2005) When Censorship is Pointless	46
FROM GEORGIA TO ROMANIA: A CHAT WITH JEFF BURR	48
THE COMICS CODE OF 1954	60
THE RUBBER THAT RUBS YOU OUT: KILLER CONDOM	63
THE OPEN CENSORSHIP OF PROFESSIONAL WRESTLING	87
A LOVE LETTER TO THUNDER ALLEY (1985): JILL SCHOELEN	109
THE RIAA'S LIST OF RECOMMENDATIONS	116
I'D BUY THAT FOR A DOLLAR!	117
ALSO FROM HAPPY CLOUD MEDIA, LLC	124

Publisher
Mike Watt:
Editor-in-Chief
Ally Melling:
Editor
Carolyn Haushalter:
Asst. Editor
Gianna Leonne:
Transcription
Robert Waldo Brunelle, Jr.:
Sage

Contributors:
**Dr. Rhonda Baughman
Justin Channell
Jason Paul Collum
Mike Haushalter
Jason Lane
Bill Watt
Justin Wingenfeld**

Cover and Art Direction:
Ryan Hose

Special Thanks to:
**Gorman Bechard
Jeff Burr
Jörg Buttgereit
Alex Cox
David Gregory
Lloyd Kaufman
Linnea Quigley
Thomas Edward Seymour
Jill Schoelen
Martin Walz**

Exploitation Nation is published periodically by Happy Cloud Media, LLC, (Amy Lynn Best and Mike Watt, PO Box 216, Venetia, PA 15367). Exploitation Nation Issue #11 (ISBN 978-1-951036-23-2) is © 2021 by Happy Cloud Media, LLC. All rights reserved. All featured articles and illustrations are copyright 2021 by their respective writers and artists. Reproductions of any material in whole or in part without its creator's written permission is strictly forbidden. Exploitation Nation accepts no responsibility for unsolicited manuscripts, DVDs, stills, art, or any other materials. Contributions are accepted on an invitational basis only. **Visit us at www.exploitation-nation.com, Facebook.com/ExploitationNation, and www.happycloudpublishing.com.**

All photographic and artistic content copyright the original holders and is included here for promotional purposes only. No rights are implicit or implied.

MR. BRUNELLE EXPLAINS IT ALL!

Please join us in welcoming renowned cartoonist, painter, author, and inventor Robert Waldo Brunelle, Jr., to the pages of *Exploitation Nation*!

DOWN THE RABBIT HOLE

It's a new year, and with a new year comes new additions to America's culture wars. I'm sure you've heard about them. Dr. Seuss was cancelled. Pepé Le Pew was cancelled. The Muppets were cancelled. This was cancelled, that was cancelled—everything was "cancelled."

It must be true. Everyone is saying so.

Of course, this ideology stems from several dumb sources, chief among them being right-wing pundits who invent this shit to distract from other things. In the case of Pepé Le Pew, the heads of FOX wanted to draw attention away from an FBI hearing into the Capitol insurrection. A blogger had commented that a scene in which Pepé Le Pew was held accountable for his decades-long sexual harassment was removed from the upcoming, for-some-reason remake of Space Jam. That was it. The blogger noted the scene, made some sort of comment about our pungent chevalier, and moved on. The right-wing news-vomit spun that into "They're cancelling Pepé Le Pew!" This devolved into shouting matches with bro-dudes wondering what the problem was and young women revealing they'd been groped by peers "pretending" they were Pepé. Just like that, people began fighting over a cartoon character none of them had watched or even thought about in years. The scene was cut for time and pacing. It'll be on the inevitable Blu-ray, which can renew the fight later.

Yes, Speedy Gonzales was brought up too. I caught a 30-day Facebook ban for pointing out that Speedy Gonzales was actually invented to battle the bigoted stereotype of the "lazy Mexican" (The lack of quotes did me in on that post). Depending on whom you talk to, Chuck Jones created Pepé Le Pew (in "Odor-able Kitty," 1945) to either poke fun at fellow animator Tedd Pierce, who considered himself a ladies' man, or irritate perennially clueless producer Eddie Selzer, who didn't like Maurice Chevalier in *Gigi* and hated the idea of the French romantic.

© Warner Bros. Entertainment Inc. All Rights Reserved.

As for Dr. Suess, this one is almost as ridiculous. *Last year*, Dr. Seuss Enterprises decided to *cease publishing* six of the author's older books—the ones you usually find remaindered or covered in dust in less-frequented libraries. The books weren't yanked from the shelves, and they weren't hurled onto bonfires. You can still have them with lox, fox, sox, in a box—whatever the fux. They just will not be published *in the future* because they contain a dozen or so images of…extreme racism. "This is the Chinaman who eats with his sticks" and the African-*like* natives behind bars in the zoo are both examples.

In his adult-oriented work, Seuss, aka Theodor Geisel, was primarily a satirist. He was also a product of his time. Some of his cartoons for adult audiences, including some of his advertising and nearly *all* of his World War II propaganda, were anti-fascist topped with levels of racism: buck-toothed Japanese, snarling Italians, etc. Sometimes, this trickled into his child-specific stuff, particularly in his imaginings of far-off places filled with people whom young Americans couldn't understand. So there are natives with hoops through their noses and Asians in coolie hats, as well as rajahs, pachas, etc. That stuff should remain in history.

Of the six books, *And to Think That I Saw It on Mulberry Street* (1937), *If I Ran the Zoo* (1950), and *On Beyond Zebra!* (1955) are likely the ones people remember best (if they remember them at all). We're not talking *The Cat in the Hat* (which was inspired by minstrel acts), *How the Grinch Stole Christmas* (which was inspired by Seuss's own hatred

"The Chinaman who eats with sticks!" From *"And to Think That I Saw it on Mulberry Street."* © Dr. Seuss Enterprises. All Rights Reserved.

of other people…I'm kidding), or even Ted Cruz's favorite Capitol floor literature, *Green Eggs and Ham*. Will you miss *McElligot's Pool*, *Scrambled Eggs Super!*, or *The Cat's Quizzer*? You will? Good news: You can still buy them from Amazon.

Maybe the images could have been redrawn. Maybe a Muppet-style warning could have been added to a foreword in each book. Regardless, Dr. Seuss Enterprises pulled the books, not mouth-frothing, woke liberals. Ergo, it was a business decision, much like Pepé.

Perhaps the biggest idiocy came from a gut reaction to Disney+. After an eternity, Disney managed to clear most of the music rights for *The Muppet Show*. This was a big deal to many of us. For too long, *The Muppet Show*—seasons 4 and 5 in particular—were unavailable. Now they are available, with a couple of caveats and two exceptions: Brooke Shields and Chris Langham.

Shields stars in an episode-long

adaptation of *Alice in Wonderland*. There are some music issues, more so than in other episodes, it would seem, as the entire episode is unavailable. The rationale is that because the show ends with "We're Off to See the Wizard" and MGM refused to grant the rights to the song, the whole episode was killed rather than rendered unintelligible. (Though Disney removed the entire plot of the Don Knotts episode to do away with "Lullaby of Birdland," so what do I know?)

The Langham episode is dodgier. A head writer on the show from Season 3 on, comedian Langham was found guilty in 2007 of downloading and possessing images and video of child pornography. He appealed, and his sentence was reduced to six months. Langham denies he's a pedophile and insists he had the images due to a part he was researching. Whatever. It's probably best to keep this episode away for a while.

Is this censorship? Maybe. At best, it's a cowardly business decision, particularly when you take into account the thing that had *everybody* mad for no apparent reason: Disney+ decided to run the following disclaimer in front of 18 episodes of *The Muppet Show*.

"This program includes negative depictions and/or mistreatment of people or cultures. These stereotypes were wrong then and are wrong now. Rather than remove this content, we want to acknowledge its harmful impact, learn from it, and spark conversation to create a more inclusive future together."[1]

This call for unity, this explanation—some would call it a warning—offended so many people so violently that it defies logic.

The "flagged" episodes (And it's the Muppets, for Chrissake, so no, there is no use of the N-word or any other slurs [though "gypsy" gets flagged at least three times as near as I can figure]) contain generally

[1] "Stories Matter." *The Walt Disney Company*, Disney, https://storiesmatter.thewaltdisneycompany.com/.

Screenshot from the "maybe-we'd-be-better-off-leaving-this-one-out" Chris Langham episode of The Muppet Show. All related images (C) Henson Associates / ITC Entertainment. All Rights Reserved.

Screenshot from the "maybe we could blur the flag out?" Johnny Cash episode.

mild stereotypes: Arabs eager for oil, Italians with their "boom-a, boom-a," narrow-eyed Asians speaking pidgin English, and Mexican lobsters speaking bandito.

But then there are bits like Joan Baez singing "The Night They Drove Old Dixie Down" (because "Pull the Triggers, N*ggers" was featured on *Lemmings*) and Johnny Cash and the entire company performing in front of Confederate flags—stuff that was "fine" in the '70s. At least it can be argued (and it will be) that in the '70s, non-whites were finally permitted at the table, at last allowed to be part of the conversation, though the ground gained was hardly equal to the ground yet to be claimed.

"They've cancelled the Muppets!" people in the present screamed.

NO. No, asshole, they did not. *The Muppet Show* is right there, for the first time in decades since Nickelodeon lost the licensing rights. *It's right fucking there!*

Cancelled means "no longer available." The Seuss books are available. The Muppets are available. Pepé Le Pew is *still fucking available.* He even has his own DVD set, all 18 cartoons. As mama might have said, knock yerself out.

I expect better from people in this end of the muck we call "the industry." I also expect better from people who've spent years actually battling *legitimate* cancel culture: voting rights being squashed, women's bodily autonomy being denied, minorities being murdered left and right. Black Lives Matter doesn't mean "your life doesn't matter, non-black person," but that seems to be the knee-jerk reaction.

Disney's warning must sure seem like a personal attack, judging from the responses: "I love Johnny Cash, so this warning must mean I'm a bad person!" Also, "Oh, no! My kids can read, and now I have to explain to them why 'greedy Arabs' are a stereotype. Next, they might ask me why Miss Piggy is such a bully!"

I've seen both. Mostly, people scream, "It's so stupid!"

"It's so stupid," you see, to care about the feelings of others, because, clearly, that's the lesson the Muppets have taught us.

"I'm not offended by it," says the mostly white, mostly male audience. Then comes the unspoken second clause: "Therefore, no one should be offended." It's not my right to tell someone they should or shouldn't be offended by something. If you are, you are. But that is not this argument. This argument is: *Someone was hurt by this, and we as a society should give a shit and try to do better*. Hence, discussion is necessary.

However, instead of discussing, we get mad at the message. Are we addicted to outrage, or are we just suckers for it?

Are warnings "censorship"? Can a pundit really be said to be "silenced" if he won't shut up on any platform? See, words have meaning. "Cancelled" doesn't mean what you think it means. Sometimes, it's a business decision. Sometimes, it's a reaction to changing society. Go back in time, call a white man a "humbug," and see if you don't get your teeth kicked in. Nowadays, it's funny. In the future, it may again cease to be funny.

To progress as a society, we have to really stop and think about how we treat each other. As was discussed ad nauseam in the last issue of *EN*, the "everyone is too sensitive" ideology is no longer a valid argument against racist jokes, nor can it beednor can punching down be calleded "satire".. "That's the way it's always been" is an invalid argument for maintaining an insensitive status quo.

The MPAA is a self-censoring system designed by those in the film industry (to an extent) to protect films against official government censorship. The Comics Code Authority was the same: a preemptive strike. Creating their own no-no rules on a sliding scale enabled industry heads to cut censors off at the pass. They are both imperfect systems, rife with their own bureaucracy and bullshit, but they're better than the Senate telling you what you can and can't enjoy.

The FCC is a different animal in that it's federally regulated, but like the MPAA, the FCC's relevance is declining rapidly thanks to the rise of streaming services. It also goes through its own bouts of hysteria. Prior to Janet Jackson's "wardrobe malfunction" at the 2004 Super Bowl, nudity and profanity were surging on network television. The Moral Minority spoke up, and the FCC found itself exercising greater authority than it had since the '50s. Then, that power declined again.

Public opinion…nebulous "community standards"…"We the People…." Is it censorship when the community says, "We won't take it anymore"?

It depends on the community.

The truth is that it only seems like we're in a bigger culture war than ever before. Because of the Internet, we're louder now. Censors like to change terms and partners (It's not "censorship" when they do it, and it's "cancel culture" when it's done to them), but it's the same old shit.

Though the quote is often attributed to Ambrose Bierce, it was Laurence J. Peter who wrote, "A censor is a man who knows more than he thinks you ought to."

We as a society need to decide what we should keep and what should die by the wayside. Regardless, both sides will inevitably cry, "Censorship!"

GOODBYE CARMINE

We lost Carmine on January 9, 2021.

If you're a regular reader, you know the name Carmine Capobianco. In fact, he submitted his very last essay for *EN* #10, giving us what would be his final word on comedy.

I've started and restarted writing this piece several times now, but I don't know how to say goodbye to him. He was, as I liked to call him, a *mensch*—the real deal; a stand-up guy.

I literally tripped over Carmine, spotting him in an indie film titled *Everything Moves Alone*, written by Tom Seymour. Tom gave me the hookup for what would become a life-long friendship.

While we didn't "talk" every day, Carmine, Amy, and I emailed, messaged, texted, and shared stupid jokes with each other on a weekly basis. For a while, we worked on a script: a pseudo-sequel to *Psychos in Love* that involved a very funny "speed dating" scene and then devolved into zombies, werewolves, and mad scientists. We were having a good time pitching jokes and ideas. The script never went anywhere, and we'd bug each other for having never really worked together yet.

That *yet*, man. It's the *yet* that gets you.

The following is the very first interview we sat down to do, back when I worked for a Texas-based newspaper called *GC*. This is where the friendship started, back in 2001.[1]

PSYCHOS IN LOVE WITH MOVIES: A BADLY TITLED INTERVIEW WITH CARMINE CAPOBIANCO

About 10 years ago, I was introduced to a movie called *Psychos in Love*, which I was convinced had been made just for me. It was about a pair of immensely likable psychopathic killers who fall in love and team up to mutually fulfill their obsession with murder. It looked like it had been made for $13, and while the acting was hardly Oscar-worthy, the two leads, played by Carmine Capobianco and Debi Thibeault, had this wonderful chemistry and comic timing and truly brought out the best in each other. Even better and more telling that this movie was made for

---

1 *GC*, which stood for *Gentleman's Club*, was a newspaper with a circulation limited to Dallas/Fort Worth strip clubs. At the time, it was edited by now-famous filmmaker Jon Keyes. I was originally hired in '99 to do book reviews. Jon turned me loose on the indie horror scene and let me write whatever I wanted. This interview was one of the things I wanted.

and partner in an independent film company called Hale Manor Productions. The company produced the very mature low-budget film *Everything Moves Alone*. Capobianco is listed as a coproducer of the company's insane and hilarious *Thrill Kill Jack in Hale Manor*. His roles in both *Thrill Kill Jack* and *Everything Moves Alone* are small but funny, conveying the same easy-going energy he displays in his previous works.

"I was actually on a soap opera—I was on *One Life to Live*," Carmine says, bringing his career up to date. "And I did a video with Tommy Shaw; I did some extra work. But I haven't been really searching for anything. Things come across my path, and I'll do them if they seem to be fun. But unless you're a major star, you can't make any money. So, I do it for fun. It's always been for fun. God knows I didn't make much money from *Psychos* and *Galactic Gigolo*."

me was that the script was completely riddled with references to old movies, some amazingly obscure. It ripped off the Marx Brothers as often as it could. For the ultimate film geek with a healthy appreciation for no-budget talent, watching *Psychos in Love* is heaven.

Psychos in Love was directed by Gorman Bechard in 1987. He, Capobianco, and Thibeault went on to make two more movies together, *Galactic Gigolo* and *Cemetery High*. Neither of these later efforts managed to capture the magic and gleeful insanity of *Psychos*, though the two leads continued to work beautifully off each other despite the lesser material.

Enter Tom Seymour, a screenwriter

Obviously, Capobianco decided that the aforementioned Hale Manor films were two "fun" things to do. In "real life," he is now a businessman and co-owns the independent video rental chain Funstuff Video[2]. A laundry list of connections brought Seymour and Capobianco together, and the younger filmmaker made his pitch for Carmine to appear in *Thrill Kill Jack*.

While Capobianco has chosen to concentrate on his business these last several years, he retains his love for movies, particularly the older classic comedies made by the Marx Brothers

---

[2] Carmine's Funstuff Video closed in the early '00s when the rest of the indie video rental stores went belly-up, first chewed up by Blockbuster and then Netflix.

and Abbott and Costello. The stores he runs in Waterbury, Connecticut, are practically overstocked with classic films. He is also the president of the Classic Movie Cinema, a grassroots movement to show today's children older movies—to show them just what today's movies have been ripping off.

"We're trying to get kids interested in the history of motion pictures and get them to watch things that were done before 1990, because there's so much crap coming out of Hollywood," Capobianco says of Classic Movie Cinema. "We have a real weird selection at Funstuff. I'm a terrible businessman and could probably learn a few pointers from Blockbuster; something doesn't rent, you dump it, get rid of it, stick it in the used bin…. Fill that space in your store with something that does rent. But I'm of the opinion that 'if you build it, they will come.' We have stuff here that rented once, if that. Now all the other video stores in the area recommend us if they don't have a particular title."

Capobianco still has fond memories of *Psychos in Love*. "In fact, about two days ago, I got another fan letter from someone who quoted some lines from it, lines I'd never thought were very funny, but they touched him in some weird way. It must still be on a lot of people's minds too. I'd read recently someone comparing *Psychos in Love* to *Scary Movie*, and you can't [make that comparison]. *Scary Movie* was just blow-job joke after blow-job joke. *Psychos* had a few blow-job jokes, of course, but it also had references to other movies, and we ripped off the Marx Brothers, etc. At West Connecticut State University, they show the movie every once in a while, and I go up [and talk about making it]. The professor there thinks it's great because he gets all the references!"

Psychos was the result of a growing friendship between Capobianco and director Bechard, who was fresh out of film school when they met. "Around 1988, I had a photo studio that I added a modeling agency to. [Gorman] was doing a video for some band, and he was looking for a model who had a very specific look, so he called me up and gave me the specifics. I said, 'Come on down.' As we got to talking, he told me that he was going to make a short film based on a short story written by another friend of his. The more we talked, the more we discovered we had in common, and we decided to make a full-length. We did a movie called *Disconnected*. I wasn't an actor—and, of course, I'm still not an actor. But he decided

to give everyone on the crew a part just for fun. So, I got to play a cop. And when the film was shown, people really liked that part; they had a lot of fun with that. We sold *Disconnected* and got, oh, about…nothing for it. We sold the rights to Taiwan—the video rights—for about $50. It wasn't a great moneymaker.

"So, [Gorman] borrowed some money from his dad so we could do a video feature. He had a script, and we took it through some rewrites, which is how we started writing together. We did a movie called *And Then…*, which was a big piece of crap. It really was. It didn't go anywhere; I wasn't proud of it at all. We showed it on a few local cable-access channels. One of the ones in Connecticut sent me a letter saying that I was nominated for a Best Supporting Actor award. And I thought, 'Wow, that's pretty cool.' And I ended up winning! So, then, Gorman said, 'Let's do another movie, and you star in it—because you're doing so well!' We came up with the idea and did *Psychos*."

With Carmine as the male lead, Bechard cast his then-fiancée, Debi Thibeault, in the role of Kate, the female mass-murderer and love interest. The resulting movie, *Psychos in Love*—rife with in-jokes, sight-gags, black humor, gore, and nudity—had it all. It is *the* movie for film buffs.

"We decided to do something that was totally off the wall, totally fun," says Capobianco of the film. "So, he wrote the first draft, gave it to me, I punched it up, and I gave it back. He'd go over it, take out some of my stuff, give it back, and I'd put it all back in. We did this for two weeks. Then, we got friends together and

Carmine as Eoj in Galactic Gigolo.
Image courtesy Carmine Capobianco.
All Rights Reserved.

shot it on weekends. And there was a lot of ad-libbing, a lot of 'Hey, let's shoot another scene because we have this great location.' It was really an incredible amount of fun doing that movie, because we didn't play by any rules. We broke the fourth wall, we talked directly to the camera, we showed the microphone at one point…. We just goofed around and put it on film. There was one scene that involved a misunderstanding between a few characters, and the dialogue was cracking us up. And because we couldn't keep a straight face, we'd have to keep doing it over and over and over. It took place in a bar, and I'm behind the bar wearing these stupid Hush Puppy shoes that would squish on the wet plastic floor mat, and that would crack Gorman up behind the camera. So, we're cracking up over the dialogue, and he's cracking up at my shoes going 'squish.' Finally, we decided to just do the scene and take whatever we got. And to this day, whenever I see that scene, I cry. It was just so much fun."

Once done, *Psychos* played numerous midnight circuits to much success. "[It] played at the Bleecker Street theater for what seemed like forever. We had a lot a lot of press come. And I don't know if it's true, if one of the reporters made it up, or if it was made up by someone we'd hired, but I heard that during one of the screenings, a woman had thrown up in her pocketbook. Then, when we went to see it at a busy midnight showing, after the first 10 or 15 minutes, people walked out! But those who stayed ended up enjoying it. I don't think it was that gory, but the gore was part of the black humor, and not everyone gets black humor. *Variety* hated it. They wrote a review saying that we just ripped off *Eating Raoul*. But we didn't. We ripped everyone else off."

With the movie working well in New York, Bechard decided to try his hand in L.A. "[Producer] Charlie Band—he loved it," says Capobianco. "He ended up buying it with the stipulation that we do four more pictures for him. And that was great! We could do them on 35mm now. He had us do *Galactic Gigolo*, which was awful. Then, we did *Cemetery High*, which was worse. All through this, Gorman was butting heads with Charlie Band over this and that, and ultimately, those two pictures were all we made."

While I do believe that *Galactic Gigolo* is also a lot of fun, I must agree with Capobianco that it really isn't a good movie. Again, what saves it from being a complete throw-away is his chemistry with co-star Thibeault. What brought an end to the trio's partnership, however, was *Cemetery High*.

"*Cemetery High* is a totally different movie from the script. It was originally called *Teenage Slasher Slut* and was a very dark comedy. There were no 'hooter honks' or stuff like that, and it was very funny, more along the lines of *Psychos*. But

"Do you?" "Do I?"
Courtesy Gorman Bechard.
All Rights Reserved.

Gorman and Charlie were butting heads again, and I got caught in the middle in a lot of ways. So, a lot of my scenes were cut because they were too dark. I was a burned-out hippie, and my wife and I would roll joints the size of basketballs—it was very funny. But then it lost a lot of its charm when it went into reshoots. *Cemetery High* wasn't even released by Charlie Band; it was released by Unicorn Video because Empire—Charlie's company at the time—went belly-up.[3]"

The end of Empire Pictures meant the end of the contract for a fourth picture. The cast and crew all went their separate ways. "Most of the people that I liked from that period went on to do bigger and better things. Actually, Eric Lutes, a guy we really liked on *Psychos*, went on to play Del on *Caroline in the City*. George, our special-effects guy, went on to work on things like *Jumanji*. He's not getting too much work now that everything is computer-generated, but for a while, he was all over the place. Gorman is writing novels and directing again. Debi got married and has a family now. Everyone's doing pretty decently. I still get fan mail all the time. I've got people coming to my store just to meet me, and I find that so flattering. I believe the rights [to *Psychos*] are still owned by Charlie Band. I've talked to Gorman over the Internet, and he thinks that in 2002, they're going to do a DVD of the movie and have Gorman and me do a commentary for it, which would be

My favorite photo of Debi and Carmine on the set of Psychos in Love. Courtesy Gorman Bechard. All Rights Reserved.

so much fun because there's so much behind-the-scenes stuff that people don't know about."[4]

Capobianco is still acting, though, in a Connecticut cable-access show called *Fun Stuff with Carmine*. "It's a local cable-access show that we do for fun. So, I took over [another show called *Land of the Free*], and we changed the name of it, and we've been doing it for three years. It's a lot of fun. It's like a night out with the guys. We do it live, and we just hang out and smoke and curse, talk about body parts, and fart. It's just fun. We have a lot of viewers, a lot of loyal fans. Every once in a while, we'll do a special show, and even though it's video rather than film, we still do some creative things. Last Halloween, I came up with this story; it was about this person who killed children on Halloween. We did it documentary style, used old photographs, and used actual locations in the town and stuff. We made it very realistic. If you

---

3 Band has since gone on, of course, to found Full Moon Features, which created the very popular *Puppet Master* franchise.

4 That happened. In addition, Vinegar Syndrome put out a handsome Blu-ray of *Psychos in Love* in 2017.

were in on the joke, it was hysterical, but if you didn't know, it was actually pretty frightening. We called it 'The Boogeyman.' We showed it the Thursday before Halloween, and the feedback we got at the station was confusion, panic. 'What's going on here? There was nothing in the paper about all this!' Then, we showed it on Halloween night, and because it was only 20 minutes, we then went on live to take phone calls about the show, and people would call up and say, 'We went on *Amazon.com* to get more information about these killings, and we can't find anything!' We pulled the wool over everyone's eyes! To this day, people think it was real. We've showed it a couple of times since then. Dee Snider [of the band Twisted Sister], who does a radio show in Hartford, had a guy call up to talk about all the killings going on every Halloween in Waterbury. It was incredible, the amount of coverage we got. They're using it at one of the colleges here to teach how media can change the course of history."

Capobianco loves to entertain— that much is obvious. He's an easy-going guy, just as he comes off in his movies. He's also literate and very funny. But he is aware of the uncomfortable trend of lost history in this country. Founding Funstuff Video with his partners was a way for him to combat the growing trend.

"I've had kids coming in looking for an old movie, and I'd recommend something from the '40s, and they'd say, 'No, no, it was out last year.' I was really sick and tired of these kids coming in and trying to get *American Pie*, which is really not age-appropriate for a 10- or 11-year-old kid. I'm not a prude, obviously, but my big thing is to let a kid be a kid. You don't have to keep exposing him to these things. He's going to end up being desensitized to violence, desensitized to sex—think that sex is okay at any age. [The problem is] kids don't want to see anything that their friends aren't watching. I have a friend who works at one of the other stores, and she has two boys, and the younger one wants to be like his older brother. He only wants to watch what Andrew is watching. And I really don't recommend that she bring some of those films home [for the younger one].

"I tried an experiment: I have three wonderful daughters, and I said, 'Listen, I'm going to bring home a movie, and we'll sit down and watch it together. I'll surprise you.' So, I brought home *The Best of Abbott and Costello*. And they wrinkled their noses and said, 'Who are these guys?' But we sat down, and they *loved* it. So, the next week, I brought home [*Abbott and Costello*] *Meet the Invisible Man*, because that's one of the few of their movies that actually has a good story. And they loved that. And the next week, I brought home *Buck Privates*. Before long, they're reading the books I have on them, and the girls are doing 'Who's on First?' and having a really good time of it. Now, my eight-year-old knows who the Andrews Sisters are. We'll go into stores and look through posters, and she'll go, 'Look, there's Marilyn Monroe! Look, there's James Dean!' People are amazed—'How does she know all that?' And I want to say, 'Because I don't let my kids watch all the crap your kids watch.'

"So, I think it worked for them. They sprang from my loins, but maybe there are exceptions to the rule. Now, kids come in, and I'll say, 'Look, take this movie. I'll give it to you for free! All you have to do is watch it, and when you bring it back, let me know what you thought of it.' I started giving away more Abbott and Costello, and the kids started falling in love with it. They had no idea who these guys were. Now, A and C weren't the greatest comedians who ever lived, but they're funny, they're entertaining, and they're very family-oriented. A kid can watch it, and an adult can watch it and still laugh. 'Who's on First?' is one of the most fun routines of all times. After getting all these kids hooked, I thought, 'Well, now I have to do this on a bigger scale,' so I started Classic Movie Cinema, which we're trying to raise money for.

In October, we did *Abbott and Costello Meet Frankenstein*. On New Year's Eve, we did *It Came from Outer Space* in 3-D. In March, we did *Camille*. Between reels, I'd get up and give information and history about the movies—let people learn a bit about the stuff. For *It Came*, we had a whole 3-D display—original posters, a display of View-Masters, 3-D comics—stupid stuff that would explain how 3-D works. It was an education/entertainment venue, and we had a lot of fun with it. We want to get a theater open so kids can see the movies the way they should be seen: on the big screen, in a darkened theater. Not that there's anything wrong with video; that's my livelihood. But it's just totally different seeing these movies in a theater."

And what film fan can argue with that, really?

Carmine (center) with ExNat editor Mike Watt and publisher Amy Lynn Best. Photo taken by Tom Brunner at Cinema Wasteland, 2017.

STOP READING, STOP BREATHING

By BILL WATT

I was amazed when, recently, I reviewed a list of the "top 100 most banned and challenged books." I was stupefied, not at the number of them that I had read, but rather, the number that I hadn't! Out of the 100, I had read fewer than two dozen! I have often been accused of being a contrarian by family, friends, coworkers, and sundry—people whom I've known over the course of 75 years—and it's a handle I've always embraced. I frequently seek out books that have controversy attached because I think every voice should be heard, every opinion considered, every point of view examined. I've read books by and about people I despise, people whose attitudes and philosophies I abhor, and I've weighed those books on the same scale I use to evaluate works related to those I admire and revere. I allow no one—*no one*—to tell me what I can read.

I was fortunate to grow up surrounded by books. When I was little, my mother read to me every night, often reading the same books over and over because I had favorites, just as every kid does. And so, my love of reading was formed early on. Mom belonged to almost every book club of the 1940s and '50s, with the exception of the *Reader's Digest* condensed classics (She always wondered what they were condensing). She favored historical novels: Thomas Costain, Lloyd C. Douglas, Frank Slaughter, and Frank Yerby, among others. If she wanted to know more about a given historical period, she borrowed books from the library. And so, I made my first connections with fiction and history and, by extension, a lifelong devotion to libraries.

Quite a few years ago, I overheard a conversation while I was browsing a bookstore. There were two women, both of whom I took to be in their fifties or sixties, discussing Harlequin romances. They were engaged in scanning the shelves and recommending titles to each other. They had little notebooks that seemed to consist entirely of Harlequin titles with checkmarks indicating, I supposed, either books they had read or books they had collected. While I shamelessly eavesdropped on them, a clerk in the same aisle as me muttered something about banning "those damn books." I asked him why he felt that way, and he told me he felt the romances were a waste of paper and shelf space and that only "old ladies" and "pimple-

Original and appropriate caption: "Hitler Youth members burn books." Photograph dated 1938. World History Archive. All Rights Reserved.

faced teenaged girls" read the stuff. He elaborated on his disdain and said that he would eliminate most genre fiction, including: Westerns ("old guys"), mysteries ("middle-aged women"), science fiction ("geeks"), horror ("weird college kids"), and what he called "straight" fiction (because all of it made people live in "fantasy worlds" and gave people "bad ideas"). When I asked him about his own reading tastes, he freely admitted: "I don't read much apart from sports biographies." It was one of the most depressing assessments of books and the people who read them that I've ever experienced.

I recently read the 60th-anniversary edition of Ray Bradbury's *Fahrenheit 451*. It posits the idea of an America of the future in which books are not only banned, but illegal to possess. The inhabitants of this imagined America live in a relentless state of entertainment, with many walls featuring huge television screens. No books exist because books make people think, and thinking makes folks unhappy. The novel grew out of Bradbury's fear that free speech was being challenged and threatened by the likes of Joseph McCarthy and the House Un-American Activities Committee, both of which investigated communism in the entertainment industry and generally and specifically targeted actors, directors, writers, and musicians. For an extended number of years, many actors, writers, and the like were prevented from working, not necessarily because of the prevalence of communism, but because of the *perceived* threat.

In essence, "cancel culture" is nothing new. And that is the very core of this very rotten apple.

Let's set one matter straight: We will never all agree on anything that won't offend someone. Have you ever read *The Adventures of Huckleberry Finn*? How about *To Kill a Mockingbird*? *Of Mice and Men*? The Bible? *Ulysses*? Here's the easiest one: Have you read the *Harry Potter* series? If you haven't, don't be upset; most of the people who have wanted them banned at various times haven't read them either! Are the books offensive? You betcha. Do racial slurs, violence, witchcraft, masturbation, adultery, unpunished murder, the physical and sexual abuse of children, rape, and gambling offend you? If the answer to all of these is yes, then, by all means, avoid the Bible. If morality, courage, loyalty, friendship, **self-sacrifice**, intelligence, and humor matter, you'll find it in abundance in all the previous titles. Here's the rub, though: Your life will change if you read and absorb what you're reading, and to do that, you will have to think. Twain, Lee, Steinbeck, Joyce, and many others aren't blowing on the soup for you; your tongue will get singed and your mind will expand, and when that happens, so will everything. You'll be transported, enthralled, upset, repelled, and changed forever. We only get one life of our own, but books allow us to live hundreds, even thousands of lives. More than any other art form, books become uniquely ours. I remember sailing with Long John Silver, facing down the evil gunman Wilson with Shane, fighting the French Navy with Horatio Hornblower, and going down the mean streets with Philip Marlowe. I've sat in the gardens in Athens and listened to Socrates and Plato, gone along with Lewis and Clark to the Pacific, and witnessed the action on Little Round Top. There are too many adventures more to count.

The future that Bradbury anticipated has not come to pass… yet. That said, the dangers to free speech and book banning seem to be operating with full vigor, just not in the same way. My greatest fear is not legislated book banning; the American Library Association has always stood between us and the "community standards" advocates who would take books away. With the proliferation of personal computers and cell phones, we hold in our hands the accumulated knowledge of virtually all known human history, and yet, we do little with it. We seek tidbits of *information* all day long, but nothing of any real substance—factoids to impress each other. But knowledge, we willfully ignore. When we utter them instead of noncommittal grunts, words, when misused, gain credibility. Even the Oxford English Dictionary now tells us that "literally" can be used as a synonym for "virtually." They exchanged *knowledge* in Alexandria. When a ship docked there, all books/scrolls were surrendered so that the librarians could copy them. The copies were returned to the shipmaster, and the originals remained in Alexandria.

Books mattered.

> "Until I feared I would lose it, I never loved to read. One does not love breathing."
> — Harper Lee, *To Kill a Mockingbird*

TOP 100 MOST BANNED AND CHALLENGED BOOKS: 2010-2019

The American Library Association's Office for Intellectual Freedom (OIF) has been documenting attempts to ban books in libraries and schools since 1990. The OIF compiled this list of the most banned and challenged books from 2010 to 2019 by reviewing both the public and confidential censorship reports it received.

Although this list draws attention to literary censorship, it provides only a snapshot of book challenges. About 82–97 percent of challenges remain unreported, estimates the OIF, which compared results from several independent studies of third-party Freedom of Information Act (FOIA) requests documenting school and library book censorship with the information in its database.

The OIF offers direct support[1] to communities to defend their right to access information. If you're able, please consider donating[2] to the OIF to ensure this important work continues.

1. *The Absolutely True Diary of a Part-Time Indian*, by Sherman Alexie
2. *Captain Underpants* (series), by Dav Pilkey
3. *Thirteen Reasons Why*, by Jay Asher
4. *Looking for Alaska*, by John Green
5. *George*, by Alex Gino
6. *And Tango Makes Three*, by Justin Richardson and Peter Parnell
7. *Drama*, by Raina Telgemeier
8. *Fifty Shades of Grey*, by E. L. James
9. *Internet Girls* (series), by Lauren Myracle
10. *The Bluest Eye*, by Toni Morrison
11. *The Kite Runner*, by Khaled Hosseini
12. *Hunger Games*, by Suzanne Collins
13. *I Am Jazz*, by Jazz Jennings and Jessica Herthel
14. *The Perks of Being a Wallflower*, by Stephen Chbosky
15. *To Kill a Mockingbird*, by Harper Lee
16. *Bone* (series), by Jeff Smith
17. *The Glass Castle*, by Jeannette Walls
18. *Two Boys Kissing*, by David Levithan
19. *A Day in the Life of Marlon Bundo*, by Jill Twiss
20. *Sex Is a Funny Word*, by Cory Silverberg

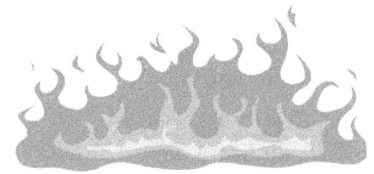

1 http://www.ala.org/tools/challengesupport/report
2 https://ec.ala.org/donation/OIF-0000-INTELL

21. *Alice McKinley* (series), by Phyllis Reynolds Naylor
22. *It's Perfectly Normal*, by Robie H. Harris
23. *Nineteen Minutes*, by Jodi Picoult
24. *Scary Stories* (series), by Alvin Schwartz
25. *Speak*, by Laurie Halse Anderson
26. *A Brave New World*, by Aldous Huxley
27. *Beyond Magenta: Transgender Teens Speak Out*, by Susan Kuklin
28. *Of Mice and Men*, by John Steinbeck
29. *The Handmaid's Tale*, by Margaret Atwood
30. *The Hate U Give*, by Angie Thomas
31. *Fun Home: A Family Tragicomic*, by Alison Bechdel
32. *It's a Book*, by Lane Smith
33. *The Adventures of Huckleberry Finn*, by Mark Twain
34. *The Things They Carried*, by Tim O'Brien
35. *What My Mother Doesn't Know*, by Sonya Sones
36. *A Child Called "It"*, by Dave Pelzer
37. *Bad Kitty* (series), by Nick Bruel
38. *Crank*, by Ellen Hopkins
39. *Nickel and Dimed*, by Barbara Ehrenreich
40. *Persepolis*, by Marjane Satrapi
41. *The Adventures of Super Diaper Baby*, by Dav Pilkey
42. *This Day in June*, by Gayle E. Pitman
43. *This One Summer*, by Mariko Tamaki
44. *A Bad Boy Can Be Good for a Girl*, by Tanya Lee Stone
45. *Beloved*, by Toni Morrison
46. *Goosebumps* (series), by R.L. Stine
47. *In Our Mothers' House*, by Patricia Polacco
48. *Lush*, by Natasha Friend
49. *The Catcher in the Rye*, by J. D. Salinger
50. *The Color Purple*, by Alice Walker
51. *The Curious Incident of the Dog in the Night-Time*, by Mark Haddon
52. *The Holy Bible*
53. *This Book Is Gay*, by Juno Dawson
54. *Eleanor & Park*, by Rainbow Rowell
55. *Extremely Loud & Incredibly Close*, by Jonathan Safran Foer
56. *Gossip Girl* (series), by Cecily von Ziegesar
57. *House of Night* (series), by P.C. Cast
58. *My Mom's Having a Baby*, by Dori Hillestad Butler
59. *Neonomicon*, by Alan Moore
60. *The Dirty Cowboy*, by Amy Timberlake
61. *The Giver*, by Lois Lowry
62. *Anne Frank: Diary of a Young Girl*, by Anne Frank
63. *Bless Me, Ultima*, by Rudolfo Anaya
64. *Draw Me a Star*, by Eric Carle
65. *Dreaming in Cuban*, by Cristina Garcia

66. *Fade*, by Lisa McMann
67. *The Family Book*, by Todd Parr
68. *Feed*, by M.T. Anderson
69. *Go the Fuck to Sleep*, by Adam Mansbach
70. *Habibi*, by Craig Thompson
71. *House of the Spirits*, by Isabel Allende
72. *Jacob's New Dress*, by Sarah Hoffman
73. *Lolita*, by Vladimir Nabokov
74. *Monster*, by Walter Dean Myers
75. *Nasreen's Secret School*, by Jeanette Winter
76. *Saga*, by Brian K. Vaughan
77. *Stuck in the Middle*, by Ariel Schrag
78. *The Kingdom of Little Wounds*, by Susann Cokal
79. *1984*, by George Orwell
80. *A Clockwork Orange*, by Anthony Burgess
81. *Almost Perfect*, by Brian Katcher
82. *Awakening*, by Kate Chopin
83. *Burned*, by Ellen Hopkins
84. *Ender's Game*, by Orson Scott Card
85. *Fallen Angels*, by Walter Dean Myers
86. *Glass*, by Ellen Hopkins
87. *Heather Has Two Mommies*, by Lesle'a Newman
88. *I Know Why the Caged Bird Sings*, by Maya Angelou
89. *Madeline and the Gypsies*, by Ludwig Bemelmans
90. *My Princess Boy*, by Cheryl Kilodavis
91. *Prince and Knight*, by Daniel Haack
92. *Revolutionary Voices: A Multicultural Queer Youth Anthology*, by Amy Sonnie
93. *Skippyjon Jones* (series), by Judith Schachner
94. *So Far from the Bamboo Grove*, by Yoko Kawashima Watkins
95. *The Color of Earth* (series), by Tong-hwa Kim
96. *The Librarian of Basra*, by Jeanette Winter
97. *The Walking Dead* (series), by Robert Kirkman
98. *Tricks*, by Ellen Hopkins
99. *Uncle Bobby's Wedding*, by Sarah S. Brannen
100. *Year of Wonders*, by Geraldine Brooks

Det er

FORBUDT

å stå i vognen så lenge det finnes sitteplasser. De som ikke etterkommer påbudet blir fra idag bortvist fra vognen og straffet.

———

Das Stehen in dem Wagen

IST VERBOTEN

solange es noch Sitzplätze gibt Wer dem Gebote nicht Folge leistet, muss den Wagen verlassen und wird bestraft.

Oslo, 4. mai 1944.
Politipresidenten i Oslo.

A FEW MINUTES WITH ALEX COX

About halfway through my interview with Alex Cox—the iconic director behind *Repo Man*, *Sid and Nancy*, *Walker*, and my own personal favorite, *Straight to Hell*—I realized that we had a fundamentally different take on "punk." My take, admittedly, is from a purely observational stance. I was barely alive when punk was first defining itself in London and further finding its nebulous identity in L.A., Berlin, and New York. Cox, of course, was on the forefront of all of that.

In his book *X Films: True Confessions of a Radical Filmmaker*, which was my Sherpa through the Cox oeuvre, he takes the reader on a journey through the rise of punk. He talks about meeting Joe Strummer while shooting *Sid and Nancy*: Strummer gatecrashed a London-based wrap party, and Cox met him in the gents. Cox recognized Strummer and "his seminal punk band The Clash, whom I'd seen, soaked with spit, sweat, and white light" [live on stage]. This was, appropriately, the beginning of a long-lasting friendship, as well as a story awash with what I think of as punk.

To me, punk is more an ideal and less an aesthetic. I think of the DIY spirit of indie artists—artists working outside of "the man"—as punk. And this attitude has gotten me into trouble over and over again.

To hardcore punks like Cox, Strummer, and the other guys who were *there*, my attitude is naïve. Punk started as a refusal of old ways. Even the "free love of the hippies" was "boring and fascist." To the punks, "sex," as expressed by Gary Oldman's Sid Vicious, "is boring, boring, boring."

Indeed, *Sid and Nancy*, as presented to Cox, was as much anathema as the first project pitched: a Madonna biopic. As Cox wrote, "The producer said there was another possibility. In addition to Madonna's story, the same studio was considering making the story of Sid and Nancy, starring Madonna plus 'that actor from *Brideshead Revisited*'" (meaning Rupert Everett). "For anyone who had been vaguely into the Punk movement, this was a troubling idea indeed. The danger was two-fold: 1) the film might get made; and 2) the film would present Vicious and Spungen as exemplars of Punk, rather than sold-out traitors to it."[1]

To Cox, my point of view must have been irritating—the view of one who is a casual observer, a poseur, or worse: a fucking tourist.

---

1 Cox, Alex. Soft Skull Press © 2008, pp. 77–78.

Miguel Sandoval, Dick Rude (with cigar), and Jennifer Balgobin in Repo Man. Photos © and courtesy Alex Cox. All Rights Reserved.

But Cox has always marched to his own drumbeat. In *Walker*, which was written by Rudy Wurlitzer (who wrote *Pat Garrett and Billy the Kid* for Peckinpah) and starred Ed Harris as the infamous self-styled general who attempted to "liberate" Nicaragua, Cox inserted a number of anachronisms to draw deliberate parallels between the crazed military man and the CIA-backed, Reagan-era fuckery going on in the '80s. Critics hated it, the film tanked, and Cox became persona non grata in Hollywood. It didn't stop him. It merely slowed him down.

While *Repo Man* is a seminal film across multiple cliques, not enough attention has been given to his exemplary *Revengers Tragedy*, an adaptation of a Jacobean revenge tale beginning with Christopher Eccelston arriving in London aboard a busload of corpses. The Jacobites had a taste for punk as well, or at least their violence had the same flavor.

So too is Cox's *Death and the Compass*—an adaptation of Jorge Luis Borges's labyrinthine crime story that features Peter Boyle and the always remarkable Miguel Sandoval—a gorgeous descent into madness and manipulation.

Take a further look at Cox's post-*Repo Man* career. *Searchers 2.0* (starring Sandoval and the always marvelous Sy Richardson) is a long meditation on what artists owe each other, one that questions whether the creation of art justifies any harm inflicted on cast and crew along the way.

Yet, each time I attempted to hammer down Cox's intent, he remained as elusive as smoke. As much I as want to understand Cox—or any other artist who has my respect or admiration—I will never truly be able to do so because I have not walked in their shoes. My "punk" is not his.

But is punk intractable or malleable? It depends on whom you want to spit at.

Presented here is our back-and-forth, edited only for clarity.

Independent filmmaking, to an

underlying extent, shares the punk aesthetic: Screw authority, screw the mainstream, tell your story your way, steal the equipment, etc. Yet, on the flip side, there's a humanitarian aspect that is also shared amongst punks and artists: to try to do so without sacrificing the dignity (for whatever that's worth) of those who are helping your dreams; feed your crew, listen to suggestions, etc. In your assessment, do you feel that "punk" is still alive, whether in music or in this spirit? Is this perhaps what is embodied in Sy Richardson's Sid and Nancy *line about "spreading healthy anarchy"?*

I don't think independent filmmaking necessarily shares a punk aesthetic, unless your definition of punk is extremely broad. Many independent filmmakers have no desire to screw the mainstream; they want to join it. I too would like to be in the mainstream, since I would have more financial security and access to funding for my films. But it didn't work out that way. One deals with the circumstances in which one finds oneself.

What is the humanitarian aspect of punks and artists? Are punks and artists the same? I know many punks and artists who don't seem humanitarian at all! What does dignity mean? Like in *Singin' in the Rain*—"Dignity, always dignity!" Who thinks or cares about this stuff?

Is punk alive? What is punk? Buñuel remarked that Surrealism wasn't just an "artistic" movement, but an attempt to change human society, and as such, it completely failed. Punk falls into that category, I think, as does Sy's character in the methadone clinic.

"*Don't look in the trunk!*" © *and Courtesy Alex Cox. All Rights Reserved.*

For good or ill, all reviewers study a body of work in search of patterns, perhaps seeing ones that aren't there, while entirely missing others. Watching your work, I've seen the aversion to authority, and possibly the idea that authority, as a body, should be held to a higher responsibility than the individual (for example, in your interest in revenge tales, but without regard to the Jacobean ideals of manifestation of sin). "Sin" doesn't seem to matter in your tales of "morality" so much as the idea that the individual can be just as destructive as the authority (and certainly has the potential to be as foolish). Is this humanitarian disappointment (a more mature but similar response to the punks and their "boring world") with a touch of nihilism?

There's the word "humanitarian" again. What do you mean when you use it? For me, it conjures up the term "humanitarian intervention" and a bunch of bombs raining down on Serbia or Afghanistan or Libya or Iraq or some other lucky recipient. I can't think of a worthwhile use for the word, it is so thoroughly devalued. Maybe the worst sin is the one identified by Thomas Aquinas: the failure to educate yourself about wickedness because you'd rather be comfortably ignorant. I don't think a lot about good and evil because most things in daily life fall into a grayer area. Of course, war and cruelty and species extinction are evil, but they are beyond my capacity to influence. A filmmaker can point out hypocrisy and double standards, though.

With Tombstone Rashomon, *you took a well-known point of history (albeit the facts of which are muddy to those outside of historical study) and presented it just as it was presented to the world—in very much that Kurosawa style of mismemory and possible deliberate obfuscation, which I appreciate. My main curiosity involves the framing "time travel" device, which leaves the ending oddly tapering. What was the intention of this device?*

Why not? If we'd had the budget, we would have shot the time machine as well, but it had to be left to the imagination!

Looking at your body of work, which began with the DIY "anything for the film" attitude (illustrated by the little old lady wanting the phone during the Repo Man *shoot), to your line-in-the-sand Q&A battle at the end of* Searchers 2.0, *one could say your perspective evolved over time. Yet, as the director, your voice remains largely neutral as to whether one should side with Mel or Fred. Again, I feel (and please correct me if I'm mistaken) that morality is for you a human issue and not a secular one. So, I ask now, where does Alex Cox stand on the morality of filmmaking, indie or "mainstream"?*

I don't understand what you mean by human versus secular. Human as opposed to animal? Secular as opposed to religious? The highest morality, by now, is the precautionary principal: the obligation to make sure that people and the environment don't get hurt and you don't leave a mess behind you when you go. This can be observed by independent and dependent films, though the latter, having more money, will tend to waste and break more things.

To clarify, I was using "humanitarianism" in the strictest sense: a single thought toward humanity, or other humans. I wasn't thinking about it in any larger sense than that. The punk scene I've been exposed to is very small, but in terms of filmmaking, the punk "aesthetic" sometimes stops and ends with Troma fans. But those with the largest antiauthoritarian attitudes are the ones I see working in soup kitchens and volunteering at homeless shelters. A few self-identified "punks" dear to me were on the frontlines of the many protests last summer. But I now realize my experiences are obviously very distilled examples of what punk is. I suppose I think of it with a very different definition.

I think both words—"humanitarian" and "punk"—have been debased by misuse and co-optation. They both meant something at one point, but I'm not sure they do any more.

Over the last two decades, the world as a whole seems to have grown angrier, grown more hostile and bitter, and been driven farther apart by the technologies we invented to bring us closer. This negativity spawned a pair of hateful buffoons who took over the governments of both of your home countries. We got to see the rocks move and the Nazis return, no longer bearing the ironic swastikas of the punks, but the genuine swastikas of the Nazi punks who will no longer fuck off. Though it now seems (irrationally, we know) that we might have some breathing room, with the Trump era and the hate-fest that is the Internet, how do you remain inspired?

Uh…orange man bad! Nazis bad! Was that the right answer?

The election of politicians you describe as hateful buffoons—in the U.S., the U.K., Brazil, and elsewhere—was enabled by those countries' mass media and intelligence agencies, who simultaneously managed to wreck the political projects of Sanders, Corbyn, and Lula. So, all is going entirely to plan.

You mention that you never felt like a director until Walker. *I feel (as many others do) that* Walker *was the culmination of what came before. I love* Straight to Hell—*I write to it, I teach it. It is very much its own animal. But* Walker *is, of course, really about something. The increasingly anachronistic touches felt very organic. While the Buñuelian surrealism is certainly a touchstone of your work, I have often considered it closer to the magic realism of Márquez, particularly in the way your characters*

The Clash's Joe Strummer in Straight To Hell. Photograph © and courtesy Alex Cox. All Rights Reserved.

often ignore the fantastic. Do you lean more toward surrealism or the natural fantastic?

I don't know the latter concept, so can't say. I think I figured out the directing thing on *Straight to Hell* because it was a more intimate and specific show, and I didn't have the benefit of a super-professional AD department.

*I've long wanted to discuss Spaghetti Westerns with someone who also understands and appreciates the American Western. While the American Western and samurai films share similar moral codes, I've felt that the Spaghettis were always more akin to the morale of Italy immediately following the fall of the fascists. In the American Western, the hero is usually the only man who can set things right for the sole reason of doing right (*3:10 to Yuma, *the execrable* High Noon—*even* The Searchers *to* a degree, although Ethan's intentions are the central argument). In contrast, the Spaghetti hero often arrives already damaged—already beaten or humiliated—and the revenge that follows, bearing inevitable destruction, is done not in the name of justice, but as a, to be blunt, reclamation of manhood. What draws you to either and both?

The landscape! The deserts of Monument Valley in John Ford films, and the Tabernas Desert in Leone's, and those fragile wooden structures surrounded by immense spaces. Chris Frayling goes into Leone's relationship with the Americans in post-war Italy in his book [*Sergio Leone:*] *Something to Do with Death*.

There are the obvious exceptions of Sid and Nancy (Yes, they were losers, but you showed exceptionally well that they loved each other in whatever twisted way they were capable), as well as Ed Harris breaking down beside Marlee Matlin's coffin (in as brilliant a performance as he's ever given). Yet, you've often struck me as more of an intellectual director than an emotional one. Not that your characters' emotional needs aren't addressed—they just often seem secondary to your narrative. This isn't a complaint; I was just curious as to how you saw yourself, directing-wise?

Do directors see themselves? I think directors are probably the worst people who should comment on their own work, at least if they're the creative types who develop their own projects. Perhaps Stephen Frears, who doesn't direct his "own" stuff, but directs scripts submitted by his agent, would have a distanced and nuanced view of his work.

Ed Harris is William Walker. © Walker Films Limited. All Rights Reserved.

ARE WE THERE YET? THE BUMPY JOURNEY OF DAVID CRONENBERG'S CRASH

By Justin Wingenfeld

Perhaps the most insightful observation made about the controversy surrounding David Cronenberg's adaptation of J.G. Ballard's novel *Crash* came from the filmmaker himself. While discussing British censors' multiple attempts to have the film banned in the U.K., Cronenberg mused that England has an island mentality and there is an ongoing effort to prevent any objectionable or impure element from gaining entry and corrupting the populace.

Certain members of the British press and government have long-standing reputations for arrogant moralism when it comes to what entertainment is allowed to be consumed by the people of England. Christian values and social conservatism were held sacred to the point of being fanatical, and they managed to weave their tendrils deep into the government and press, with public figures like Mary Whitehouse obsessively (and successfully) campaigning against anything deemed offensive or, even worse, permissive.

While this moral crusade led to blatant censorship in England (and many other parts of the world), the U.S. has proudly boasted its adherence to free speech and freedom of expression. Currently in the U.S., organizations like One Million Moms (which is really only about a dozen, and not all moms) are loud and proud about their puritanical sensibilities when it comes to entertainment, but they are rarely

Director Cronenberg. All images this section © The Movie Network / Telefilm Canada. All Rights Reserved.

taken very seriously. Censorship goes against the very fundamentals of the First Amendment, and even those members of the U.S. government who would like to control what Americans are allowed to see, read, and listen to are generally held at bay. Those who aren't subdued usually crash and burn in a heap of self-induced humiliation (think Nixon vs. Lennon or the FBI vs. "Louie, Louie").

But the island mentality of which Cronenberg spoke is not limited to literal islands, and the morality police have found more insidious ways of muzzling speech they don't like. When Cronenberg and executive producer Jeremy Thomas unleashed *Crash* onto an unsuspecting public in 1996, the film's most formative opponents would turn out to be the press in the U.K. and the film's own distribution company in the U.S.

James Ballard (James Spader) is a successful film producer. His spouse, Catherine (Deborah Kara Unger), is a housewife who spends her days taking flying lessons. It is in an aircraft hangar where we first meet Catherine having sex with a stranger; meanwhile, James is busy screwing his camera operator. Their evening is capped off with unenthusiastic sex on their balcony as they watch the highway, teeming with traffic below, and tell each other about their respective sexual encounters during the day.

That night, a distracted James gets into a head-on collision with another car. The passenger in the other car is Dr. Helen Remington (Holly Hunter), and the driver, killed in the crash, is her husband. While recovering at the hospital, James is approached by Vaughan (Elias Koteas), a mysterious, physically scarred orderly who is fascinated by James's injuries and system of pins and splints. Later, Catherine tries to get James aroused by describing the aftermath of the crash in detail to him, but she is unsuccessful.

While at the lot where both their cars were taken, James and Helen meet and have a brief discussion about their changed perception of traffic since their crash. James offers Helen a ride, and during the drive, they are almost involved in a fender bender. They are both excited and aroused by the incident and head to the parking garage at Helen's building, where they have passionate sex in James's car. That evening, James and Catherine have sex in a more enthusiastic manner than usual.

Helen invites James to a reenactment of James Dean's fatal crash, which is hosted by Vaughan and performed by professional Hollywood stunt drivers. After the presentation is interrupted by local authorities, Helen, James, and the drivers head back to Vaughan's workshop, where James meets Gabrielle (Rosanna Arquette), a woman who was severely injured in a car wreck years earlier, and discovers that she, Helen, the stunt drivers, and several other unnamed people are followers of Vaughan, who believes that car crashes are an inherently stimulating experience that awakens an intense sexual excitement unattainable any other way.

James becomes a follower, and eventually, Catherine does as well. The fantasy of James and Vaughan having sex becomes a source of extreme arousal for Catherine, who later allows herself to be ravaged by Vaughan as James sits in the driver's seat and the vehicle moves through a car wash (a scene that Ballard particularly adored, calling it "pure cinema").

Vaughan encourages James to join him at a tattoo parlor, and both get automobile-themed tattoos. Afterward, they have sex, but their encounter ends on a sour note when Vaughan becomes jealous of James's ability to get sexually excited alone in a random junked car, provoking Vaughan to repeatedly ram the car before driving off in a rage.

James then accompanies Gabrielle to a sports-car dealership, where she entices an employee to help her get inside a display car, resulting in a hook on her leg brace tearing the leather upholstery. She and James then have a sexual encounter, during which James penetrates her in the vagina-like scar on the back of her thigh, much to her extreme pleasure.

While James and Catherine are out driving, Vaughan spots them and begins following them in a threatening manner. Vaughan then intentionally drives his car off an overpass, crashing into a bus, setting both his car and the bus ablaze, and dying in the process.

Afterward, James and Catherine seek out Vaughan's car at the impound, stating that the owner was an old friend. Before James and Catherine can transfer ownership of the car, Gabrielle and Helen find it and have sex in the back seat.

Some time later, James and Catherine go out driving, Catherine in

her car and James in a Frankenstein-like combination of Vaughan's car and his own from his initial accident with Helen. He rams Catherine's car, eventually forcing her off the road, where her car overturns. James finds Catherine banged up but disappointed that she is not more seriously hurt. He consoles her as they have sex next to the overturned car.

The above synopsis is barely a simplification of the events that occur in the film. There isn't much more to the plot, and that is by design. This is not a nuanced comment on the dangers of sexual obsession or Hollywood's tendency to mix sex and violence like bacon and eggs. While there may be elements of social commentary in the film, they're never at the forefront. The characters in *Crash* are who they are, and they do what they do. They are apathetic to societal standards and only interested in their own self-fulfillment. While we as the audience may be appalled by their behavior, the film offers no concrete moral stance.

Before it was published in 1973, Ballard's novel faced resistance from appalled prospective publishers, one of whom boasted that Ballard needed

psychiatric help. Literary critics reacted similarly once the novel was published. The *New York Times* called the book "repulsive." The author himself has since been at a loss as to what to make of the novel or how it even came to be. Ballard called it a science-fiction story about human beings' reliance on technology. He also referred to it more generally as a "cautionary tale." He later walked back both statements.

Were Cronenberg's film adaptation indeed a cautionary tale, critics might have been more comfortable with it. *Videodrome*, *The Fly*, *Dead Ringers*, and *Naked Lunch* all had a certain morality. While all are undeniably challenging films, they at least offered the audience a life preserver in the form of an objective moral in the end, whether it was a comment on meddling with nature or a warning regarding the dangers of drugs, sex, and violence. Neither the final moments of "Brundlefly" begging for death nor William Lee's devastating realization that his existence has become a Möbius strip of drug-fueled despair can be called a happy ending.

Crash offers no such relief and forces the viewer to either attempt to relate to the characters or remain an objective observer. Neither option in this case is easy. Finding no way to connect with characters is a singularly disturbing experience. A movie that is otherwise well-made and has an interesting story can be an uncomfortable experience without at least one character for which we can root.

Crash is almost entirely ambivalent as to the behavior of

the characters, with only Howard Shore's steely, ominous score hinting at something sinister. It is this cold, detached atmosphere that prevents us from allowing the film to do the moralizing for us, and this is what the British press found so repellent. If Cronenberg had taken a more sensationalistic approach, the film might have been easier to digest and, more importantly, shrug off as a sleazy exploitation picture.

The fundamental problem was that critics like the *Daily Mail*'s Christopher Tookey—who, in a scathing review, called for *Crash* to be banned—considered the film as if it were indeed a sleazy exploitation picture. Tookey lamented the filmmakers' attempts to eroticize car crashes and bodily injury and was worried that unhinged viewers might watch the film and attempt to reenact what they saw. Tookey later wrote a follow-up defense against fellow critics who accused him of trying to force his values down everyone's throats, though it is unclear how else one could interpret a call for a work of art to be banned from public consumption.

American film critic duo Gene Siskel and Roger Ebert perfectly summed up the opposing interpretations of *Crash*. Siskel, while not worried about the dangers of copycat behavior, also expressed bewilderment at what he saw as an attempt to eroticize car crashes, and he considered the film a failure due to its inability to successfully turn him on. His cohost, Ebert, who admired *Crash*, countered that the film does not attempt to eroticize car crashes, violence, or bodily injury; it is merely *about* people who do—"crazy people," as Ebert was quick to point out. Even Cronenberg, after watching *Crash* for the first time in years, said he thought to himself, *These people are crazy!*

Regardless of what they do for their day jobs, the characters in *Crash* are, if not outright mentally ill, all broken, obsessive people living secret lives on the fringes of society. Some manage to keep up a respectable front, while others have fully embraced their psychological and physical damage, allowing it to consume their lives. Gabrielle has gone so far as to fashion her back and leg braces into makeshift S&M gear.

While what these people do is objectively destructive not only to themselves but to innocent bystanders caught In their path, none of them ever has that moment of clarity to ease the audience's discomfort. If even one of the characters were to suddenly realize the insanity and irresponsibility of his or her actions, the viewer would have someone with whom to sympathize. But we are offered no such relief. The Ballards go from being cold, bored people keeping their sex life interesting through risky extramarital trysts, to being a pair of psychopaths in need of the most extreme stimulation just to get aroused.

Yet, the filmmakers do not expressly tell us how to feel about it. We may be appalled watching James fuck Gabrielle's leg scar, but at that moment, for the two of them, it is the most obvious thing in the world to do. The closest thing to objective morality is being allowed to witness the mayhem and pain Vaughan and his followers cause the innocent people around them.

When Vaughan, James, and Catherine come across a multicar accident during a nighttime drive (and get a closer look due to Vaughan posing as an accident photographer), they discover the accident was caused by Seagrave—one of Vaughan's stunt drivers—in his attempt to recreate Jayne Mansfield's tragic vehicular demise. Vaughan's own fatal crash results in unquestionable death and/or injury as passengers flee the wrecked bus, which is engulfed in flames. Even Gabrielle's accidental damage to the car seat causes the salesman obvious dismay.

Regardless of the severity of damage they depict, the previously described scenes are thoroughly uncomfortable to experience, especially since there is no subsequent catharsis. No one ever has to pay for their "sins." If the manager of the car dealership came out and berated Gabrielle, or James flipped the bill for the damage to the seat, we would get a moment of relief. Vaughan and Seagrave both die; neither is held accountable for the death and destruction they've caused.

Cronenberg wants to make us squirm, and so we are left to stew over the unresolved mess that is left behind, resulting in subtle but unrelenting tension. A dazed victim of Seagrave's Mansfield reenactment barely even registers as an opportunity to sympathize with someone, as the focus of the moment is Catherine taking in the spectacle around her.

It is this spectacle that so worried Tookey and others in the British press that they called for the film to be banned, lest kids get up to auto(mobile)erotic mischief on the way home from the theater. Even before the film was slated to be released in the U.K., Cronenberg, Ballard, and Thomas were attacked by British film critic Andrew Walker following a screening of the film at the Cannes Film Festival. Cannes was followed by a lengthy campaign against the film in the British press and government. Hundreds of articles and multiple front-page stories about the crime against humanity that is *Crash* appeared in conservative British newspapers.

Their efforts were largely unsuccessful. Even the censor-happy British Board of Film Classification (BBFC) could find no legitimate reason to ban or even cut the film, acknowledging that *Crash* was an allegorical exploration of thrill-seeking and the increasing need to push limits in the face of societal desensitization. A psychologist hired to determine if the film was likely to cause copycat behavior concluded that the detached and unpleasant presentation of both sex and car crashes in the film was enough to void any excitement that might inspire people to mimic what was shown on-screen.

In a bizarre act of desperation, the opposition screened *Crash* for a group of people with disabilities, assuming the group would find the film offensive enough that a case could be made that it was psychologically harmful to people with permanent injuries. Again, no such luck, as the group was unanimously ambivalent to the film's portrayal of the disabled. In fact, the implication that Gabrielle continues to be sexually active and desirable despite her injuries was generally viewed by the group as a positive thing.

In the end, thanks to the efforts of cinema licensor John Bell and conservative politician Virginia Bottomley (neither of whom bothered to see the film), *Crash* was banned in the Westminster district of London. This was a largely symbolic bone-throw to the detractors, as it did little to prevent anyone who wanted to from seeing the film.

Ultimately, the BBFC gave *Crash* an 18 certificate (the equivalent of an MPAA NC-17 rating), and the film was released, uncut, in March 1997. *Crash* should have received an October 1996 release in the U.S. (as it had in Canada), but coincidentally, it was not released in U.S. theaters until the spring of 1997. This time, media mogul Ted Turner was the major roadblock.

Cannes proved prophetic of the American controversy when jury president Francis Ford Coppola expressed his disdain for *Crash* and refused to personally give Cronenberg the Special Jury Prize, an award created specifically for *Crash* due to its "daring" and "audacity." The film was ultimately picked up for distribution by Fine Line Features, the art house division of New Line Cinema, which had recently been acquired by Turner Broadcasting Systems, which, in turn, had just merged with Time Warner.

New Line was no longer the "House That Freddy Built"—a haven for independent films, horror movies, and edgy comedies. It was now the house that Ted Turner owned, and while the intention had been to allow New Line to continue to operate as it always had, the extreme nature of *Crash* was more than even as liberal-minded a businessperson as Turner could bear.

Turner was appalled by *Crash*. Like Tookey, he was concerned that teens might watch the film and attempt to recreate it while making out in the driver's seat and going 75 miles per hour on the highway. Turner pulled the film from release and kept it shelved until finally allowing its release six months later. The impetus for his change of heart remains unclear but may simply be Turner's revelation that he was withholding the film due to his own personal distaste for it. Upon announcing that the film would finally be released, Turner made it clear that he wasn't happy about the

release. At the same time, he tried to downplay the motivation behind the delay by claiming he did not want *Crash* getting lost in the holiday movie rush…in October.

In the wake of *Crash*'s release both in the U.K. and U.S., there was no rise in automobile accidents specifically caused by Vaughan wannabes. The film opened to mixed reviews and modest box office returns, which was not bad for a film weighed down by the dreaded NC-17 rating. While U.S. audiences may have been vaguely aware of a controversy surrounding the film, the British press had made it its mission to beat readers over the head with the insistence that they were far too delicate to handle such depraved garbage.

But unlike *Make Them Die Slowly* or *Snuff*, *Crash* was not some microbudget sleaze-fest that could wear its "banned in 37 countries" status like a badge of honor. It was a multimillion-dollar production from a respected filmmaker who had financiers and stockholders waiting for their investments to pay off. Perhaps the advertising campaign could have leaned a more sordid direction, but that would likely have alienated the art house audience. It would have also antagonized the thrill-seeking crowd, who would have been attracted to the seedier approach.

When the film eventually made its way to home video, both Blockbuster and Hollywood Video refused to carry the NC-17 version, or even an unrated edition. They insisted on an R-rated cut, which was ultimately delivered in the form of a choppy, nearly incomprehensible mess missing about 10 minutes of footage that, in true U.S. fashion, almost entirely comprised sex and nudity.

Other than a New Line Home Video DVD, which included both the R and NC-17 cuts, and a Criterion Collection laser disc of the NC-17 cut (both released in 1997), *Crash* was scarcely available on home video for more than 20 years. Finally, in December 2020, Arrow Films in the U.K. and the Criterion Collection in the U.S. each put out its own special-edition Blu-ray and DVD releases of the film. At last, fans got the opportunity to see a remastered edition of Cronenberg's film in all its twisted-metal and scarred-flesh glory.

What is *Crash*? A cautionary tale? Science fiction? The blackest of black comedies? A deliberately extreme freak show simply meant to shock? Ask different people and you're likely to get different answers. That is the challenge of *Crash*. While its story is fairly straightforward, its motivation is ambiguous. You're likely to take away from it what you bring with you.

And maybe that is what people found so disturbing: not only the dark recesses of their own minds, but more frighteningly, the minds of their peers. To them, *Crash* represented a rabbit hole leading to the depravity locked away in all our psyches, a depravity that, once unleashed, would infect society as a whole. Little did they know that it was their own fear and paranoia that would, ironically, prove to be the true sickness.

Conservatives and puritans need their boogeymen. In the 1950s, it was communism. In the 1980s, it was satanic ritual abuse. And for a little while in the mid-90s, it was *Crash*.

DEAR SANTA, THIS YEAR I'D LIKE YOU TO GO AWAY... MIDWEST MOMS VS. BILLY

BY JASON PAUL COLLUM

It's responsible for quite possibly one of the biggest moments of public disdain and protest over a film, only possibly outcried by *The Last Temptation of Christ* (1988). In November 1984, *Silent Night, Deadly Night* slayed its way into theaters.

The film depicts an 18-year-old orphan wearing a Santa suit and losing his cookies in response to a traumatic childhood moment. He is clearly not Santa. His name is Billy. He's rather handsome, very fit, and before killing people, a very gentle soul. Today, the controversy seems to be remembered as surrounding the film itself, but the fact is that the true gasoline was the trailer, which sent Midwest moms into an unhinged fury.

It all began the week prior to the film's release, when the station under contract with theatrical distributor Tri-Star chose an unfortunate time to air the commercial: between super saccharine *Little House on the Prairie* and sketch comedy *Three's Company*. The majority of the trailer does not distinguish the key piece of the plot: The killer *isn't* Santa. Instead, the trailer leads one to believe that Santa has, in fact, gone nuts. Ax in hand, chopping through doors, terrorizing screaming girls, his face barely seen—this is Krampus, and he's out to "punish." Only at the tail end of *one* of the TV spots does the narrator announce, "He only looks like Santa Claus."

I must admit that at 11 years old,

this commercial terrified me. My days of believing in Santa were long gone, but I still recall the commercial in vivid detail, and I remember thinking that, in fact, Santa had become a madman. My love for horror had not yet arrived, so any TV trailers featuring a slasher scared me. TV spots for *Friday the 13th Part III* (1982) and *Return to Horror High* (1987) were in league with that *Silent Night, Deadly Night* trailer, emblazoning my psyche before I covered my eyes. In that regard, the commercial had done its job: That trailer, especially to a child, was scary. A nation of June Cleaver moms took notice—and they were pissed.

The first protest in America began at my back door, in Milwaukee, WI. TV images of protestors outside the now defunct theater the Grand filled the local nightly news. The group—Citizens Against Movie Madness—had written signs that read, "Save Santa," "We love Santa," "Santa is sacred," and "Shut this movie down all over our town!" Two days into the film's release, newspapers began covering the protests, and the controversy quickly spread to national news outlets. In short form, parents—with their minors tagging along—began hitting theaters throughout the Midwest. *Daily Herald* journalist Dann Gire wrote a scathing commentary on the trailer specifically, stating, "In 30 seconds, they effectively turn [Santa] into a bearded, bloodthirsty boogeyman."[1]

Initially, Tri-Star saw dollar signs. One of Hollywood's most common beliefs is that controversy draws curiosity seekers; therefore, there's no such thing as bad publicity. Ever since the massive successes of the unholy trio *Halloween* (1978), *Friday the 13th* (1980), and *Prom Night* (1980), major studios had been snatching up independently produced slashers, although the golden era of the slasher film, 1978–1984, was nearing its end by the time *Silent Night, Deadly Night* was released. The weekend of its release, *Silent Night, Deadly Nigh* was up against *A Nightmare on Elm Street*, and it initially outperformed the Freddy Krueger classic. Tri-Star's initial plan was to release its slasher—which it had hoped would become its franchise—in a few Midwest towns and then slowly spread it outward to the coasts and bigger cities, where Tri-Star expected the film to reach a wider audience. After all, "trashy" and "sleazy" horror films were

---

[1] Kerswell, J.A. "Ho-Ho-Homicide: The *Silent Night, Deadly Night* Controversy." *Hysteria Lives*, https://www.hysteria-lives.co.uk/silent_night_deadly_night/

commonplace in big cities, especially on the coasts. However, this was not the case in the Midwest. Dreams of a franchise were dashed as protestors grew stronger and began to find their movement was working.

Critics took notice too. As is typically the case when the opposition is asked their thoughts on a movie, the response was most often, in a tone of offense, "Well, I haven't actually seen it!" Unfortunately for Tri-Star, newspaper and TV critics did go, and their words were scathing, not only regarding the reason why the protestors were gathering, but regarding the quality of the film itself. "The degenerates that make these movies should be exterminated"[2] seems the most powerful. Gene Siskel and Roger Ebert, who had deliberately ruined the finale of *Friday the 13th* as a form of protest against slashers, carried their anger on air, declaring, "Shame, shame, shame…. Your profits are truly blood money."[3]

Ultimately, however, it was those first-week audience members anticipating a level of terror from *The Texas Chain Saw Massacre* (1974) who shut the movie down. Made for $750,000, *Silent Night, Deadly Night* drew in a quick profit, but its tired clichés, minimal scares/suspense, and basic gore (minus Linnea Quigley's impressive impalement on deer antlers) were old news. It's undeniably a cult classic beloved by many an anti-Christmas film-goer today, but by the end of its two-week initial run, *Silent Night, Deadly Night* had brought in only $2.5 million. (Compare that to *A Nightmare on Elm Street*'s impressive $24 million, earned at the same time.)

Tri-Star played stupid and began distancing itself, saying it was pulling the film from theaters due to low profits ($2.5 million in 1984 did not qualify the film as a failure). Even though Tri-Star had sent out promo materials with the headline "A Christmas Stalking from Tri-Star," the company began acting ashamed of what it had released and tried to bury the film. It even went so far as to try to deny producer Ira Barmak's offer to buy the licensing rights back (He eventually succeeded and put the film back in theaters for a short run in July 1985).

Moms self-declared their war won. Due to a combination of protests and poor attendance, some theater owners pulled the title before Tri-Star's actions. In December 1984, the Catholic Church held a special conference in New York to discuss *Silent Night, Deadly Night* in particular, declaring the film "an abomination." Horror fans and journalists found it amusing that the Church was still attacking a film that had not played in theaters for three weeks. Some complained that the critics at the conference had likely not even seen the film due to this fact. Coincidentally, specific elements from the film were never mentioned at the conference.

In the end, nearly four decades later, the myth of the controversy surrounding *Silent Night, Deadly Night* has only made its fan base stronger. A franchise ultimately ensued through IVE/LIVE (now Lionsgate). *Silent Night, Deadly Night Part 2* (1987) follows

---

2 Kerswell.
3 Bailey, Jason. "He Knows When You've Been Naughty." *Vulture*, Vox Media LLC, 24 Dec. 2018, www.vulture.com/2018/12/how-silent-night-deadly-night-inflamed-a-nation.html.

(created by Screaming Mad George) that put actress Neith Hunter through FX hell. It's also considered by many to be the best-made, with much thanks to director Brian Yuzna. The final sequel, *Silent Night, Deadly Night 5: The Toy Maker* (1991) steals from *Pinocchio* (1940), *Dolls* (1986), and *Puppet Master* (1989). It finds its own notoriety from the appearance of Mickey Rooney, who had written an infamous article in 1984 about the travesty of a film like *Silent Night, Deadly Night* existing.

Billy's younger brother, Ricky, on his own hunt for nasty Mother Superior, who tormented and abused Billy. This sequel became a cult classic in its own right due to an over-the-top performance by lead actor Eric Freeman, culminating with his "Garbage day!" line. *Silent Night, Deadly Night 3: Better Watch Out!* (1989) was the best-looking but most subdued entry. It is notorious for Ricky (here played by *The Texas Chainsaw Massacre Part 2*'s Bill Moseley) wearing a bubble cap on his head to cover his exposed brain as he chases a blind girl with whom he's become infatuated (à la 1968's classic *Wait Until Dark*). *Silent Night, Deadly Night 4: Initiation* (1990) is essentially an unrelated story, with Ricky, played by Clint Howard (who reprises the role in *Part 5*), as a minor character. *Initiation* is a wickedly entertaining series of gross-out witchcraft moments

It should be noted that none of the sequels, nor the film's 2012 theatrical remake, raised a moment of controversy, including *Part 2* (the only other entry that came out in theaters). Other killer Santas and Christmas-themed horrors existed long before, such as *Tales from the Crypt* (1972), *Home for the Holidays* (1972), *Black Christmas* (1974), *Silent Night, Bloody Night* (1972), *Christmas Evil* (1980), *To All a Goodnight* (1980), *Don't Open Till Christmas* (1984)... the list goes on, even more so today. None of these films seemed to raise an eyebrow.

What's often forgotten in the legacy of *Silent Night, Deadly Night* is that it wasn't the film's actual content that was controversial, even landing the title on the U.K.'s "Video Nasties" list and "banned" lists in other countries. It was merely a 30-second TV spot, played between two popular family-hour shows, that rocked not just the nation, but the world over.

THE MOTION PICTURE PRODUCTION CODE
(AS PUBLISHED 31 MARCH, 1930)

A CODE TO MAINTAIN SOCIAL AND COMMUNITY VALUES IN THE PRODUCTION OF SILENT, SYNCHRONIZED AND TALKING MOTION PICTURES

Adopted by Association of Motion Picture Producers, Inc., at Hollywood, Calif., and ratified by the Board of Directors of Motion Picture Producers and Distributors of America, Inc., March 31, 1930.

Reasons for the New Code

The advent of sound on the motion picture screen brought new problems of self-discipline and regulation to the motion picture industry. Sound unlocked a vast amount of dramatic material which for the first time could be effectively presented on the screen. It brought the dramatist to Hollywood, to supplement the work of the scenario writer. It brought stars from the legitimate stage and the variety stage to the talking motion picture screen. It brought spoken dialogue, which had to be adapted to the requirements of film presentation. It brought new "extras," many of whom were given spoken lines.

To meet this new situation it became necessary to reaffirm the standards under which silent films had been produced since 1922, and to revise, amplify and add to those principles in the light of responsible opinion, so that all engaged in the making of sound pictures might have a commonly understandable and commonly acceptable guide in the maintenance of social and community values in pictures.

The task undertaken by the Motion Picture Producers and Distributors of America, cooperating with educators, dramatists, church authorities and leaders in the field of child education and social welfare work, has now resulted in the adoption of a new Code by the Association of Motion Picture Producers.

The new Code has been accepted and subscribed to individually by such prominent producers in the motion picture industry as: Art Cinema Corporation (United Artists); Christie Film Company, Inc.; Columbia Pictures Corporation; Cecil B. de Mille Productions, Inc.; Educational Studios, Inc.; First National Pictures, Inc.; Fox Film Corporation; Gloria Productions, Inc.; Samuel Goldwyn, Inc.; Inspiration Pictures, Inc.; Harold Lloyd Corporation; Metro-Goldwyn-Meyer Studios, Inc.; Paramount Famous Lasky Corporation; Pathé Studios, Inc.; RKO Productions, Inc.; Hal Roach Studios, Inc.; Mack Sennett Studio; Tiffany Productions, Inc.; Universal Pictures Corporation; and Warner Bros. Pictures, Inc.

Principles Underlying the Code

1   Motion picture producers recognize the high trust and confidence which have been placed in them by the people of the world, and they recognize their responsibility to the public because of this trust.

2   Theatrical motion pictures are primarily to be regarded as entertainment. Mankind has always regarded the importance of entertainment and its value in rebuilding the bodies and souls of human beings.

3   It is recognized that there is entertainment which tends to improve the race (or at least to re-create and rebuild human beings exhausted with the realities of life), and entertainment which tends to harm human beings, or to lower their standards of life and living.

4   Motion pictures are an important form of art expression that enters intimately into the lives of human beings. The art of motion pictures has the same object as the other arts – the presentation of human thought, emotion, and experience, in terms of an appeal to the soul through the senses.

5   In consequence of the foregoing facts the following general principles are adopted:

No picture shall be produced which will lower the moral standards of those who see it. Hence the sympathy of the audience should never be thrown to the side of crime, wrongdoing, evil or sin.

Correct standards of life shall be presented on the screen, subject only to necessary dramatic contrasts.

Law, natural or human, should not be ridiculed, nor shall sympathy be created for its violation.

Particular Applications

Crimes against the law
These shall never be presented in such a way as to throw sympathy with the crime as against law and justice or to inspire others with a desire tor imitation.

1   *Murder*
a   The technique of murder must be presented in a way that will not inspire imitation.
b   Brutal killings are not to be presented in detail.
c   Revenge in modern times shall not be justified.

2   *Methods of crime* should not be explicitly presented.
a   Theft, robbery, safe-cracking, and dynamiting of trains, mines, buildings, etc., should not be detailed in method.
b   Arson must be subject to the same safeguards.
c   The use of firearms should be restricted to essentials.
d   Methods of smuggling should not be presented.

3   *Illegal drug traffic* must never be presented.

4   *The use of liquor* in American life, when not required by the plot or for proper characterization, will not be shown.

Sex
The sanctity of the institution of marriage and the home shall be upheld. Pictures shall not infer that low forms of sex relationship are the accepted or common thing.

1   *Adultery*, sometimes necessary plot material, must not be explicitly treated, or justified, or presented attractively.

2   *Scenes of passion* should not be introduced when not essential to the plot. In general, excessive passion should so be treated that these scenes do not stimulate the lower and baser

clement.

3   *Seduction or Rape*
a   They should never be more than suggested, and only when essential for the plot, and even then never shown by explicit method.
b   They are never the proper subject for comedy.
4   *Sex perversion* or any inference to it is forbidden.
5   *White-slavery* shall not be treated.
6   *Miscegenation* is forbidden.
7   *Sex hygiene* and venereal diseases are not subjects for motion pictures.
8   Scenes of *actual child birth,* in fact or in silhouette, are never to be presented.
9   *Children's sex organs* are never to be exposed.

Vulgarity
The treatment of low, disgusting, unpleasant, though not necessarily evil subjects, should be subject always to the dictates of good taste and a regard for the sensibilities of the audience.

Obscenity
Obscenity in word, gesture, reference, song, joke, or by suggestion, is forbidden.

Dances
Dances which emphasize indecent movements are to be regarded as obscene.

Profanity
Pointed profanity or vulgar expressions, however used, are forbidden.

Costume
1   *Complete nudity* is never permitted. This includes nudity in fact or in silhouette, or any lecherous or licentious notice thereof by other characters in the picture.
2   *Dancing costumes* intended to permit undue exposure or indecent movements in the dance are forbidden.

Religion
1   No film or episode may throw ridicule on any religious faith.
2   Ministers of religion in their character as such, should not be used as comic characters or as villains.
3   Ceremonies of any definite religion should be carefully and respectfully handled.

National feelings
1   The use of the Flag shall be consistently respectful.
2   The history, institutions, prominent people and citizenry of other nations shall be represented fairly.

Titles
Salacious, indecent, or obscene titles shall not be used.

Repellent subjects
The following subjects must be treated within the care and limits of good taste:
1   Actual hangings, or electrocutions as legal punishments for crime.
2   Third Degree methods.
3   Brutality and possible gruesomeness.
4   Branding of people or animals.
5   Apparent cruelty to children or animals.
6   Surgical operations.[1]

FILM RATING CODE HISTORY

G (1968-Present)
M (1968-69)
GP (1969-71)
PG (1971-Present)
PG-13 (1984-Present)
R (1968-Present)
X (1968-90)
NC-17 (1990-2018)
X-18 (2018-Present)

---

1   "Appendix 1: The Motion Picture Production Code (as Published 31 March, 1930)." *Arizona State University*, Arizona Board of Regents, www.asu.edu/courses/fms200s/total-readings/ MotionPictureProductionCode.pdf

Satirical photograph staged in 1940 by Paramount photographer A. L. "Whitey" Schafer, that illustrates the "Commandments According to Hays." The image itself was submitted to the judges of 1941's Hollywood Studios' Still Show - all of whom were outraged and refused the poster to be exhibited. © A.L. "Whitey" Schafer. All Rights Reserved.

LINNEA QUIGLEY'S CHRISTMAS STALKING

BY JASON PAUL COLLUM

For nearly 40 years, actress Linnea Quigley has been seasonally stalked by her most infamous film, *Silent Night, Deadly Night* (1984). Scooted off to Salt Lake City, Utah, in the winter of 1983, a then little-known ingenue was a year away from the film that made her a household name: *The Return of the Living Dead* (1985). She'd had supporting roles in a number of independent horror films, such as *Psycho from Texas* (1978), *Graduation Day* (1981), and *The Black Room* (1982)—all of which had come and gone with little fanfare. However, she was known amongst producers as an adorable, petite blonde who was willing to disrobe on camera.

This was her job on *Silent Night, Deadly Night*. Teenage girl Denise (Quigley) messes around with her boyfriend, Tommy (Leo Geter), on the basement pool table. As soon as each has popped their tops (Both of their exposed torsos serve for some forthcoming gore), Denise's pussy… cat meows at the door, and off she goes, topless, to open said door and give the nearby carolers an early gift. No sooner does her pussy jump through the door than psycho Santa Billy Chapman (Robert Brian Wilson) bursts through as well, axe in hand and ready for some Christmas Eve carnage.

Job completed, Quigley moved on to other films. Ironically, it was on the set of *Treasure of the Moon Goddess* (released in 1987 and Quigley's first lead role in a comedy) that the news about that Utah gig having caused more than a little stir was broken to Quigley over a phone call.

As Quigley tells it, "I learned when my manager called me in Mexico, where I was filming. When he told me about the controversy, all I thought was, *How stupid. It's just a silly little slasher movie.* I didn't think much more of it after." When she returned to the states, however, Quigley saw the protests on television and was stunned.

"I think it was overreacting," she recalls, feeling the ensuing censorship was far from justified. Some of the footage showing the extent of her impalement had been hand cut from prints of the film by theater owners. "I think some parents wanted something besides their own kids to be mad or upset about."

For a long time, some had the notion that as Quigley's scream-queen career exploded into the later half of the 1980s and early '90s, she deliberately tried to distance herself from the film and its first sequel, which reused so much of her footage that she was given another on-screen credit as a result. (In fact, she had become the breakout star of the film she had long put behind her.) Some thought she had feared losing jobs as a result of the film's infamy. She now says she looked at it quite the opposite.

"No," she says, shaking her head. "I probably *gained* jobs, because [all of the controversy] gave the movie a name—notoriety—from the bad publicity." In fact, by the time *Silent Night, Deadly Night* reached rental stores in its first giant clamshell box through U.S.A. Home Video in 1986, and a year later through IVE for the home market, the film seemed to be in every video store in America. "I didn't try to hide it. I think I knew *Silent Night, Deadly Night* wasn't a great film, but its fame was built on controversy and negative reactions to the topic, not the filmmaking [process]. It was not great filmmaking."

She laughs again as she adds, "The guy who directed *The Adventures of Grizzly Adams*, Charles E. Sellier, Jr., directed *Silent Night, Deadly Night*! It's funny."

Quigley, who has seen her share of censorship over a 43-year career spent largely in the horror genre, has never known the "morality" device to be justified. "Censorship is weird," she says. "It depends on where the film is being released. Europe has its nonviolent rules, but sexual content is okay. It's just the opposite here (in America). I'm glad when a film gets in trouble, because then it gets free publicity, which ultimately helps so much in gaining attention [from fans]."

Indeed, Quigley is a proponent for free speech and letting individuals make their own decisions about what is appropriate viewing for themselves and their families. After a simple but assured pause, she concludes, "I would say just let people know about the content they will be seeing."

Linnea and Jason. © and Courtesy Jason Paul Collum. All Rights Reserved.

TRANSPORTER 2 (2005): WHEN CENSORSHIP IS POINTLESS

BY MIKE HAUSHALTER

Top-tier package delivery agent and militant Uber driver Frank Martin (Jason Statham) leaves southern France and takes up shop in sunny Miami. Between jobs, Frank is moonlighting as a chauffeur and bodyguard for Jack (Hunter Clary), the young son of Audrey (Amber Valletta) and Jefferson Billings (Matthew Modine), the latter of whom is a powerful pharmaceuticals CEO. When the young charge is kidnapped while in Frank's care by mercenaries attempting to facilitate a bioterrorism plot, Frank proves once again that he is a force to be reckoned with, and he kicks ass and breaks bones to keep his promises to Jack.

Transporter 2 is a high-octane Statham vehicle that is full of hard-hitting incessant violence, turbo-charged vehicular mayhem, and amusing critiques of American cuisine that are not concerned with the laws of physics. It's action-movie junk food that's a bit closer to a low-rent James Bond clone than a car chase film: It won't stick with you for long, but it's plenty tasty as you're consuming it. It's fair to say that if you're a fan of Jason Statham, you will probably like this film. While it's not as action-packed as the *Crank* outings, *Transporter 2* offers up plenty of Statham's macho charm and ample displays of on-screen mayhem.

As in the previous *Transporter* outing, Statham is supported by a decent cast of familiar, if not famous, faces, some of which include the return of François Berléand as the glib Inspector Tarconi, Modine (*Full Metal Jacket*) as a workaholic jagoff, Valletta (*Dead Silence*) as a distressed

(C) 20th Century Fox. All Rights Reserved.

and love-starved mother, bootleg Antonio Banderas aka Alessandro Gassmann (*The Dinner*) as lead villain Gianni Chellini, Kate Nauta (*Avalanche Sharks*) as a super sexy femme fatale, Keith David (*They Live*) as the ineffective head lawman, and chameleon Jason Flemyng (*The League of Extraordinary Gentlemen*) as a jumpy hypochondriac henchman.

You might be wondering why I would choose to expound upon *Transporter 2* rather than *The Transporter*, the film that more or less launched Statham's American career. It's mostly because the second film is a bit of an underdog that is slightly better in a few ways than the original. In addition, I wanted to point out that the American release of *Transporter 2* has been censored to remove and obscure scenes of nudity and bloodshed from the film; this is a fact that's really rubbed me the wrong way. In response, I, of course, had to pick up a Thai bootleg of the film, which not only included all the nudity that was too risqué for pearl-clutching American audiences to witness, but also had improved CGI effects.

Truth be told, *The Transporter* was also cut to get a PG-13 rating, but all that was removed was some violence, which meant those scenes were included as deleted-scene bonus material when the film hit DVD. Since nudity was almost all that was trimmed from *Transporter 2*, the censored material has never seen the light of day on an American release, not even as a cut scene. What is it about the sight of female nipples that gets Americans all up in arms, anyway? The footage in question doesn't even show that much nudity—just some nipples through a see-through top, and a bare butt. Still, it was enough to make me feel I was missing out if I didn't get an imported copy (two copies, in fact, since I have recently upgraded to a German Blu-ray box set that has a director's cut of the first two films).

FROM GEORGIA TO ROMANIA: A CONVERSATION WITH JEFF BURR

I'll just come right out and say it: To know director Jeff Burr is to love him. It's the reason he was able to charm Vincent Price out of semiretirement to star in the low-budget *From a Whisper to a Scream*. Burr's easygoing nature won over actors like Viggo Mortensen, Clu Gulager, Susan Tyrrell, David Warner, and countless others. In commentaries, on panels, and in conversations, he's generous with credit and praise for his disparate cast and crew. Meeting Burr, you're often of the impression that he's just as excited to meet you.

Yet, invariably, when Burr's name is mentioned by reviewers, the first thing they bring up is his penchant for removing his name from films he didn't feel delivered "his vision" (in sneering quotes).

"Listen," Burr says, wanting to set the record straight, "there's a reason: The movies that I've taken my name off were the movies where I shot them but had no presence in the editing room. When I direct a film, I have a certain way of shooting it so that it'll be put together in a certain way. And then we can discuss what works,

Director Burr at the height of fun in Romania. All photos this section © and Courtesy Jeff Burr. All Rights Reserved

have new ideas, etc. But I wanted it the way it was intended *first*, and that's the clay you're going to mold. As you know, postproduction is so important, and if you have no say in the editing, music (placement or type of music), sound effects—anything—it just makes me more and more disconnected from the process. Just FYI, I never used the credit 'A Jeff Burr Film' unless I had complete creative control over the whole thing. It's not that I want *control* in the sense—it's not a *bullying* kind of control; it's just that you want to be the filter that every idea comes through and to be the final arbiter of the movie. And you get the movie you want to make on the screen. I've gotten into arguments with producers who couldn't believe I didn't want the [authorship] credit *at all*. 'What do you mean you don't want that credit? Everyone wants that credit.' *No*. I don't want the credit. They were in disbelief.

"To be quite frank, in my entire career, I only feel like I've made three movies."

Those three, Burr enumerates, are his first feature—the aforementioned *From a Whisper to a Scream*—the tragicomic *Eddie Presley*, and the harrowing World War II film *Straight into Darkness*. Though he may be ultimately and forever best known for *Leatherface: Texas Chainsaw Massacre III*, for Burr, the three previously mentioned films come closest to bearing his stamp.

"I've never been satisfied with a movie I've directed, *ever*. The day you're completely satisfied with something you've made, you might as well retire. It'll never get better than that."

So, with 'cancel culture' freely bandied about, what is this kind of interference? "I can't say it's 'censorship,' though I will say it's stupidity. You asked the question, 'Why do they hire you?' My mindset is always, if I'm hired to make a movie, I come in and tell them, 'I see the movie as this, here's what I would do, and here's what I would bring to the movie,' and I get hired. Then, I think if I'm on schedule and on budget and the machine is well-oiled, so to speak, leave me the fuck alone. Is that too much to ask? You want all the mistakes in the movie to be your mistakes. It drives me crazy when a decision is handed down from a corporate level or *producorial* level that you can't fight, and you know it's a wrong decision that just imploded the movie…. If you know it's a mistake and your name is on it, that just kills you. I include casting in that, the final script—everything. This is going to sound egotistical, but there's not a movie that I was hired to direct that wouldn't have been better if I hadn't gotten any input from the producers and was just left alone. I mean that. To what degree they'd be better, well, that varies from the different movies. They would all be better."

This begs the eternal question writers and directors have asked producers since Aristophanes got notes from Caesar: Why would you hire a person and not let them do the job? "Exactly! I knew the business had taken a huge pendulum swing to a different level when I got basically fired—or just let go immediately after production—from a million-dollar horror movie. I'm going—this is 2005—'Motherfucker, I'm the biggest name *on* this thing,' in terms of marketing, I mean. And then I'm just unceremoniously released. They just didn't give a shit. It was never going to be a good movie, but it was going to be a *fun* bad movie instead of what it is now, which is just a *bad* bad movie. It was a very inexpensive, kind of throwaway movie. It's going here, it's going here. The stakes were so low. But this was a case of a first-time producer and a neophyte writer (being the same guy) believing that the script was sacrosanct and brilliant. In the final version of the film, it used the script line for line. Nothing is different. That's when I knew, if I can't even have any influence over a horror movie in 2005, what's left? It's been a strange bumpy ride since then.

"Bottom line is, when you're making a film, it's like Stanley Donen said: 'Making a film is a soul-crushing affair. The only thing worse is *not* making a film.' Nowadays, I can suss out a bad situation quicker. I have a certain regret of my career to date. I don't mean to make it sound more negative than it is, and most of it is my own fault. For the '90s, I kind of picked a lot of low-hanging cinematic fruit, and that was to my detriment. But I learned a lot along the way."

Let's face it: The ever-evolving film business ain't what it used to be just 10 years ago. "To be honest, the director's role in narrative filmmaking has gotten less and less and less important over the last 15 or 20 years," Burr says. "That's why you have studios hiring—you're like, 'How did this guy wind up directing this $200 million?' Well, he *doesn't* direct a $200 million movie. He's 'a guy.' There is so much more going on—the visual effects, stunt work—they'd almost rather hire a visual effects guy to direct. Something like a Marvel movie, the new Godzilla, or whatever; these younger—or rather, 'less experienced,' I guess—these newer guys—*what do they do?* I don't know. The stakes are so high in terms of money, and it's not enough for it to be a successful movie on its own. It has to spawn 10 ancillary companies and be an amusement park ride as well.

"Now, the smaller movies—those are my sweet spot. My ideal would be a $10 million. Maybe those are coming back with Amazon and Netflix, but a $10 million comedy-drama—that's the hardest kind of movie to make. It's too much money on one hand and not enough on the other. The production in Georgia is mostly in the Atlanta area and Savannah…that kind of antebellum time period—a lot of structures from that era, for period pieces or stuff. It has the relative uniqueness of New Orleans or Charleston. The tax credits here aren't going away at least. Filming has resumed in Atlanta at least, but the big stuff is driven by Marvel and Disney."

And what will be the delivery system for entertainment anyway? Thanks to the pandemic, streaming services wound up with the purse strings, and their eyes are on long-form storytelling, limited series—that sort of thing. Multiplexes across the country have closed permanently. The infamous Cinerama in Los Angeles just announced it's going dark forever...again.

"In our industry, I really wonder. It's changed forever. It's never going to be what it was in terms of just the business model or how entertainment is made or consumed. I hope I'm wrong, but I don't see a mass return, even if everything is all clear, to theaters. Broadway will return, absolutely. There's a uniqueness and immediacy for live theater and community theaters around the country. There's a deep ingrained desire to hear stories live and see performances. But with film, there's obviously going to be niche, art house places, and on the flip side of that, there will be IMAX—just the spectacle kind of thing.

"But in terms of every week a big movie opening and people going to see it in a theater, I think those days are gone. And I *hope* I'm wrong. The business model for all the major corporations is streaming now, and they're not going to change that. The day and date release will be in theaters and streaming, making it unexceptional. Theater attendance was going down anyway, even before all of this. The price of tickets was going up; people just started staying home. But in terms of just sheer numbers of people going to theaters, [attendance] was going down since the '90s—well, since the '40s, with the invention of television. Hopefully, there will always be an audience that wants to get out of the house and see a movie.

"For me, my enjoyment, or my passion, let's say, is narrative filmmaking, ideally for theaters, but for home theaters as well—not necessarily in a traditional way, but in a narrative way. Reality shows don't interest me. I understand the appeal, but not for me to make or try to get off the ground. But, like, the five-minute little thing on YouTube...I want to make 'content'—and I hate that word—but I want to make something that has a shelf life, that will last! And that is anathema to so many people in our industry. We have the gatekeepers who—how do you monetize a small independent film or a limited series on a true independent level? The only thing that I have—not 'going for me,' but...the only name recognition I have at all that you could put on something would be if I made a horror film, you could say, 'From the director of *Leatherface*' or whatever, not that that would necessarily cause a stampede to the streaming sites. Knowing the stakes for me are higher than ever—I'm of a certain age, so how many more chances am I going to get? When I do, I want to be able to take advantage of the chance and make something that I really want to do. So, that's really where I am in terms of my artistic life."

But with the absence of new projects, Burr has, like so many of us, turned to restoring some of his earlier work in hopes of finding new audiences through better-quality transfers. "I'm doing a couple of restoration things for a couple of films that I co-own, to get them to the Blu-ray physical market and to streaming, *Eddie Presley* being one of them and *Straight into Darkness* being another, and this crazy little movie called *American Hero*, which we're going to call something else. We have to shoot a couple of days on that to give it a framing device and a context. It's an action movie that is now 25 years old, shot on 16mm. It's a long story. But getting 4K scans made and finding all the elements and all that kind of crap…which is good, and I'm glad so many of us are restoring our old stuff, but you have to find a way to move forward as well. I don't want to be a fly in amber."

That being said, the idea of new viewers getting the chance to fall in love with *Eddie Presley* or descend into hell with *Straight into Darkness* (not to mention Scream Factory's gorgeous Blu-ray of *From a Whisper to a Scream* [originally released in 1987 as *The Offspring*, which Burr cowrote with C. Courtney Joyner, Mike Malone, and Darin Scott]) is exciting.

Eddie Presley, which I waxed ecstatic about in *Movie Outlaw*, is a down-to-earth story about an aging Elvis impersonator (played by the sublime Duane Whitaker, who wrote the film's source play) finally getting his big break amidst other wacky down-on-their-luck performers. The film is sad, ridiculous, marvelous, and ultimately life-affirming in the face of shattered dreams. It's also charming and subtle.

Compare that to *Straight into Darkness*, a surreal war film that likens to the horrific Russian film *Come and See* (released in 1985 and directed by Elem Klimov) in terms of horror and willing atrocity, a claim I do not make lightly. The audience follows two army deserters as they make their way across enemy land and wind up at a devastated school in which maimed war orphans fight back against the Nazis as a "game." *Straight into Darkness* earns its pedigree right off the bat, removing the viewer from the familiar "Rah-rah, go get them Nazi bastards!" rhetoric when the MPs (cameos by James Le Gros and Daniel Roebuck) who are escorting two deserters—sensitive Losey (Ryan Francis) and bestial Deming (Scott MacDonald)—run over a mine in the road. The prisoners escape on foot, and the audience goes with them, tripping from one horrible event after another.

Burr shot the film with a verisimilitude that brings the

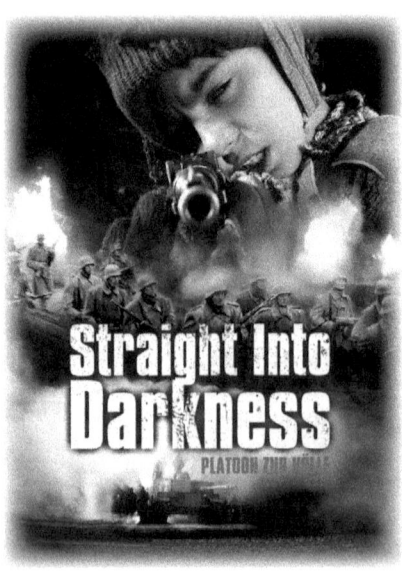

surrealism into hyperfocus. This gives the film a "you are there" feel, with strange touches in the story that could have only come from firsthand accounts. If you've ever read diaries of WWII dogfaces, you'll find the same matter-of-fact horror depicted in *Catch-22*, as well as the same gallows humor. Nothing feels distilled.

"It was an idea I'd had in my head for a long time," Burr tells me, "at least since high school. My grandfather and father, my uncles—they all served in WWII. That was always around me as a kid. WWII movies were prevalent in the '60s and '70s as well. The bare bones of the story were in my head for a long time."

Straight into Darkness began its evolution, Burr says, in 1995. He'd spent time in Romania shooting movies for Charles Band and Peter Locke during the Kushner-Locke period of Band's ongoing slouch toward Babylon. During Burr's "one off day," he was approached by a P.A. named Kostel Musat. "He goes 'Hey, I know this is a lot to ask, but could you visit the orphanage I grew up in, today? I'm sure the kids would love to meet you.' It was a lovely experience, and we all ended up going to see *Bean*, the Rowan Atkinson feature film. The children just loved that and laughed at everything. So, it was just a great day, being around those kids and stuff. And that's probably what coalesced the children's portion of the movie in my head.

"I started jotting down notes and writing stuff, and then, about six months later, I got a call from my mom asking me to come back to Georgia because my dad was sick. So, I came back and kind of helped nurse my father, who'd had a whole bunch of illnesses hit him at once. Then, he passed away. There's a saying in the South—I'm sure there are variations of it all over, and it's not *true*, but I understand the good-old-boy part of it—it's 'You're not a full, complete man until your dad dies.' That impacted me more than I ever thought it would. And it made me draw a line in the sand and do this thing.

"Because I was back in Georgia for a few months, I got reacquainted with a guy I grew up with named Mark Hannah. He was also a Super 8mm filmmaker in this area. He wanted to work on whatever independent film was gonna be my next project and produce it. The final, I guess, *talisman* in making this was that I called a travel agent and just asked how much two tickets to Romania would be in the summer, etc. The tickets were $298 each. I took that as a sign that I gotta go and just make this fucking thing. We did a location scout in Romania. And it sounds probably reckless to make a period war film in Romania, but by that time, I had made maybe four or five movies over there and had gotten to be very good friends with a director of photography, Viorel Sergovici, who—again, a sign—had formed his own independent company. So, he agreed to come onto the movie as a producer/financier/director of photography. He brought this guy, Dan Vornicu, in, as well as a whole bunch of people that he knew in high places in Romania who could pull strings and get things done. I put everything I had, pretty much, into the movie.

"We made the movie for—I think the final figure was $700,000 or something like that…somewhere around there. We shot 35mm and 16mm. We started shooting in early February of 2001.

"It was a nightmare," Burr adds with a laugh that turns into a sigh, and then he retreats. "It was a complete logistical—not nightmare, but a challenge for obvious reasons. The kids, the subject matter, everything…. It was a new production company over there, and it was totally independent. There was no master executive producer that knew exactly what had to be done on their end."

When they finally arrive at the orphanage, run by Maria (Linda Thorson) and Deacon (the marvelous David Warner), the two deserters meet the casualties of the war: the innocents chewed up by the "games" of adults.

According to Burr, working in Romania was challenging at the best of times, even indoors. Things didn't operate the way they were supposed to, which led to lapses in communication. Case in point: While the crucial role of Maria, the ersatz mother of the orphans, ultimately went to Thorson (best known for replacing Diana Rigg on *The Avengers*), Burr had originally set his sights on another '60s actress. "The first one we tried, and we sent her information via fax to France but never heard anything, was Charlotte Rampling, who probably would have been out of the price range anyway, but you never know. Anyway, I ended up having a long talk with Susan George. She loved the script, said she had a lot of ideas about it. I was initially reticent by some of the demands she had up front. She didn't want to do any nudity,

and she wanted to wear a wig instead of cutting her hair. It was like, 'You're committed, but it's *surface committed*,' in my mind, anyway. But anyway, I told her that I had some thoughts and I'd fax her soon—couple of hours or a day, or however long it was.

"In the office we were working out of, the infrastructure was very bad. At the time, certain parts of Romania were not Internet-savvy, and it was difficult at that time to make a cell phone call or even fax or email. So, days go by, and every day, I ask the secretary there, 'Did we get any response from Susan George?' 'No, no, sir, we have not.' The next day—so this five or six days later and we've gone with Linda Thorson (We had to in order to give her time to prepare, plus plane tickets to book, etc. and all that shit)—somebody is looking in the office for a blank piece of paper or something, and they turn over a sheet with the last paragraph of a fax from Susan George. And it's so beautiful, it's so heartfelt—oh my god! So, Susan George probably hates my guts because I never responded to this beautiful fax. And I never got the first pages of whatever it was! So, that's the kind of thing that happened on this movie."

Casting Deacon also came with hoops through which to jump. "I almost had John Hurt, but there was a scheduling issue. But I always loved David Warner, and he is a total consummate pro. He flies in. He asks questions, and he's marinated the material in his brain. He didn't just look at the page an hour before he shot. He's been thinking about it. But as soon as he wraps and leaves, it's gone. 'Yeah, I was in a movie in

Romania with a bunch of kids.' That's it. He just kinda wipes the memory. A lot of these guys are like that, or they might remember a bunch of things that had nothing to do with the movie. But I was really lucky to have him.

"The fondest memories I have of the movie are of casting the kids. There were four or probably five orphanages we visited in Romania to cast out of. This was before Romania put a moratorium on adopting out to foreign seekers. In these orphanages were a number of special-needs kids because Ceaușescu, the former dictator, had ordered that: Any kid with a real abnormality would be put in a state-run orphanage. They were really warehouses. It was sobering. You think you have an idea of what it would be like, and then you see the reality, and it's oftentimes worse than you imagined. But the kids there—you wanted to cast every frickin' last one of them. One very sorrowful thing: Every one, down to the boy and girl—they were all starved for attention and affection, not because their caregivers were bad, but the numbers were staggering. Casting the kids was a real special process—painful on one hand, but very enjoyable on the other. And the kids we got—it was a gift to have them all. They were just wonderful, every one of them. They really had a great time on the movie, and you can see; it's tangential to the movie itself, but it's life. Every kid—you could watch their confidence grow every day they filmed, when they would do something that was great and we responded to it. And that was just a joy to see."

The star of this little group is the legless Nelu, played by Romanian street kid Nelu Dinu. In one of the film's most harrowing sequences, Nelu is sent out into the snow to sabotage an oncoming Panzer tank. Reminiscent of both *The Big Red One* and Johnny Eck in *Freaks*, Nelu runs on his hands and hides in the brush, and the audience is on the edge with fear over what will happen. We've already seen what the Nazis do to the

The child warriors from the "Four Soldiers" segment of From a Whisper to a Scream.

healthy. But in this sequence, Nelu is the star.

"Nelu—he's a very important part of it. On the October trip (the first trip to find locations), Mark had to leave early. I was there for another week and a half, and I was walking down one of the streets at night, and there was Nelu playing soccer with a bunch of other kids—batting the ball with his hands. So, I stopped and started talking to him. We're smiling at each other and laughing, and I knew he didn't understand a word I'd said. I understood very little Romanian at the time, and even today, very limited. We were right next to the Intercontinental Hotel, so I asked the concierge there to write out in Romanian, 'Look, I need to meet you here tomorrow at noon, same place we are now. I want to talk to you about being in a film'…something like that. Nelu reads the paper, laughs, and gives me the thumbs up.

"So, the next day, I met him and, through an interpreter, explained what I wanted him to do, and he's excited—'This is gonna be so much fun. I get to shoot a gun! Great!' That was it. I found him on the street and subsequently, he's been in several movies that Castel Film Studios did [most notably, *The Wild Dogs* in 2002 and the terribly strange *Wolf Girl* in 2003]; a hell of a natural actor and forget the disability—just a fascinating guy. That was a very lucky meeting on the street. Because of that, I then wrote around him, thinking of things he had to do and scenes he had to be in."

It's difficult to watch these scenes and not draw parallels to the "Four Soldiers" story in *From a Whisper to a Scream*, in which mangled Civil War orphans bring Cameron Mitchell's Sgt. Gallen to justice. It's a shock in *Whisper*. In *Darkness*, it's tragic.

"Some people have mentioned [the similarity] too, and I don't have an answer to that. The only thing I can say is there was a *National Geographic* article about the Russian war in Afghanistan. This was '79—that was the invasion—so I was about 17. The picture was a girl, probably about nine or 10, and she was missing a leg. There was an improvised metal thing that reached the ground (so she could walk), and she had a machine gun in her hand. She was a child soldier for Bin Laden, as we came to know him much later. She was with the mujahideen. That was one of the inspirations for *The Offspring* story. I don't know. It's a thread, I guess."

For the orphans in *Straight into Darkness*, Burr does something unique, lovely, and heartbreaking: As each life is lost, Burr gives us little snippets of the children pre-war—smiling, happy, the footage shot in bright sunlight, as opposed to the desaturated ugliness of the world of their present. These 16mm moments give each character an instant backstory, if only emotionally, that is immediately ripped away as the viewer is left staring at a corpse, the dopamine still dissolving in their brains.[1]

"To put it a theatrical way," Burr explains, "I wanted to give each of the kids a curtain call. When we cut the

---

[1] Weirdly enough, it's a motif I've seen only twice before: once in a French New Wave by Alain Resnais whose title escapes me, and the other in Dennis Devine's *Vampires of Sorority Row Part II*.

first one of those, I thought it would be pretty powerful."

The initial shoot for *Straight into Darkness* was arduous, and it didn't have a satisfying conclusion. "We shot twice. One winter, in typical filmmaking fashion—every winter in Romania has snow and cold; this year, 'We've never seen a winter like this!' So, we didn't get as much snow as we wanted in the initial shoot, which was 20 or 21 days. We left Romania the first time without having shot the film. As a filmmaker, you know just how painful that is, especially in a foreign country, but if you shoot anywhere and have to leave that shoot out of necessity knowing you have not shot the movie…it means you have to get the actors back. There is no contract that shows they have to come back. And, unusual for me, I had a very contentious relationship with both leads, but one of the leads in particular. One guy was just, you know, young…loved being on location and fucking everything that moved. The other guy was a character actor who had been elevated this one time to a lead, and that kind of went to his head. That's the personality trait I get along with the *least*. But we had something that makes no sense without additional shooting. There were certain things we didn't get shot for a variety of reasons—financial, snow…all that kind of stuff. When we started to edit, we knew we'd have to regear for another shoot, and getting those two guys back was a hassle and a bit of a financial hit."

Ultimately, the second 10-day shoot accomplished what was necessary to make the film coherent. Burr had something exciting, harrowing, tragic, horrific, and special. Again, *Straight into Darkness* isn't a run-of-the-mill war film. It's its own angry, writhing beast, one tiring of the madness in its wake. As usual, Burr found that making the movie was the easy part.

"Every filmmaker has been down this road: You make a film, you put everything into it, and you think somebody is going to notice the effort and the expense and whatever. But no one on a certain level noticed it. Several times, it was like the junior executive gets excited by it, [he] shows it to the one person who can make a difference, and *he* hates it. [So the movie dies.] remember Lawrence Gordon, who was originally at AIP in the '70s. Some executive at Larry Gordon Productions got excited about *Darkness* and said, 'Larry has to see this.' Larry watches it and goes, 'What is this shit?'"

It's a rough ride, to be sure, but to work so hard and not find the right audience is heartbreaking. "This movie is very—I won't say it's divisive, but there are some people who are very affected by it. I have letters and emails and some reviews that get It, but there are others who feel that it veers into exploitation. The *Variety* review—well, I've never gotten a good review from *Variety*. [*laughs*] But they were like, 'The movie becomes an exploitation movie when the kids are trotted out as cannon fodder in the later reels.' I know there were some people in the audiences of some screenings who were upset—very into 'cancel culture' before that was a thing, with this attitude: 'How dare you exploit this disabled child! How awful, what you made him do!'…that kind of thing. And quite obviously, the opposite was true. He had a great time. His dad and whole family came to the shoot. He was treated with respect and dignity, financially too, and he became a friend. I've read that in more than one review of it, but I've also had people bring this up in panels. 'They were exploited, and…' blah, blah, blah. I don't agree with it, but I'm not going to change anyone's mind."

"Divisive" isn't always the kiss of death, especially for horror, but cross-genre is difficult to market. MCA's initial release features Deming in the foreground, pursued by skull-faced Nazis, airbrushed over stock imagery. It's a miserable bit of art and typical of the misunderstanding *Straight into Darkness* suffered.

"It was one of those movies where it rose to a certain level with some people and then died there. Same with festivals; you would think many festivals would want to book it, but not really, and especially not in America. The biggest festival we got into was South by Southwest in America, and it was programmed but a shitty venue and time. It was kind of dismissed there. I might have thought, at the time, that this will get me noticed differently than I was before. But no. [*laughs*] It was one of those rare things where desire and opportunity met in my career. The thing I'm saddened by and feel guilty about, but I'm rectifying it, is that it was the last independent movie I made. I thought it would be a start of a new career."

Still, Burr shrugs off the negative and charges ahead, daring you to jump aboard, his enthusiasm contagious. "Anyway, I'm more revved up now than I have been in a long while, and that's a good thing. But I want to make a few films that go the distance. I don't think I've made a film yet that really, really goes the distance. I've maybe come close a couple of times. But I haven't been satisfied with anything *to date*. The experiences of making the films have been…maybe *Leatherface* was the worst experience I had at the time on a set, on a daily basis." He then adds, "That had nothing to do with the actors. They were great, and so was the crew. It was just the producers and the company. It wasn't like I was right 100 percent of the time, and neither were they 100 percent wrong, but it could have been a much better, different situation. It had nothing to do with the money or the time it took to shoot. It was a personality clash in a lot of ways, certain key personnel I clashed with. I was very naïve in terms of cinematic politics. I could have been much more savvy politically, dealing with what happened with the movie."

So, what would go the distance? "That's exactly what I'm working on right now. It's been a project I've had for many years in my mind, and I'm finally getting it out. It's that $10 million comedy-drama, if you will. I can't do it for $200K. I might be able to do it for $2 million with favors. It's not like it's huge in scale, but there are certain things and performers it needs. The problem is the lead: It's an ensemble piece, but the character who would be the ostensible lead is 90 years old. There are two ways to go: a younger actor with prosthetics, or digital, like with *The Irishman*—

something like that—which would be a big hassle. It's not like there's a huge talent pool of 80-year-old actors who have that body of work behind them. Gene Hackman would be perfect."

Less-savvy readers might miss the longing all artists have for the work not-yet-made. Non-artists may not even get it. But for an artist to achieve his or her goals, honesty in self-assessment is crucial. Few of my acquaintances are as self-aware as Jeff Burr.

"This is a very old-fashioned attitude, but hell, I don't care. I really feel that you make a movie, you get it exactly where you want it or to what it should be, with all the various stages of a movie, and then the movie is finished, and it doesn't belong to you anymore. And whatever the audience gets out of it is what the movie is. It doesn't matter what my intention was. It doesn't matter what I think is good or anything. It's like a painting: You may have painted it with a certain intention, but the observer may come away with an entirely different experience…and will, because there are so many movies that I love that I experience and that I just know the people who made the movie had no fucking idea of *me* having this experience.

"It's an ego thing too. I have things in me. I know once I do a movie that represents what I think I'm capable of doing, that's the one I'll talk about frame by frame. That doesn't mean I hate everything I've done or that I disown the movies. They're all truly—and it's a horrible analogy, but it's true to me: They're pieces of your life. You can remember who you were and where you were in your life when you made them. You have a completely different mindset about them than the people who just watch the movie."

Eddie Presley got a handsome two-disc release from J.R. Bookwalter's Tempe Entertainment in 2004, and copies can still be had on Amazon. The same is true of *Straight into Darkness*. Scream Factory's release of *From a Whisper to a Scream* is also a must-have for any library.

Adieu, Vincent. (From a Whisper to a Scream still courtesy and © Jeff Burr. All Rights Reserved)

THE COMICS CODE OF 1954
CODE OF THE COMICS MAGAZINE ASSOCIATION OF AMERICA, INC.
ADOPTED OCTOBER 26, 1954

PREAMBLE

The comic-book medium, having come of age on the American cultural scene, must measure up to its responsibilities. Constantly improving techniques and higher standards go hand in hand with these responsibilities.

To make a positive contribution to contemporary life, the industry must seek new areas for developing sound, wholesome entertainment. The people responsible for writing, drawing, printing, publishing, and selling comic books have done a commendable job in the past, and have been striving toward this goal.

Their record of progress and continuing improvement compares favorably with other media in the communications industry. An outstanding example is the development of comic books as a unique and effective tool for instruction and education. Comic books have also made their contribution in the field of letters and criticism of contemporary life.

In keeping with the American tradition, the members of this industry will and must continue to work together in the future.

In the same tradition, members of the industry must see to it that gains made in this medium are not lost and that violations of standards of good taste, which might tend toward corruption of the comic book as an instructive and wholesome form of entertainment, will be eliminated.

Therefore, the Comics Magazine Association of America, Inc. has adopted this code, and placed strong powers of enforcement in the hands of an independent code authority.

Further, members of the association have endorsed the purpose and spirit of this code as a vital instrument to the growth of the industry.

To this end, they have pledged themselves to conscientiously adhere to its principles and to abide by all decisions based on the code made by the administrator.

They are confident that this positive and forthright statement will provide an effective bulwark for the protection and enhancement of the American reading public, and that it will become a landmark in the history of self-regulation for the entire communications industry.

CODE FOR EDITORIAL MATTER

General standards—Part A

- (1) Crimes shall never be presented in such a way as to create sympathy for the criminal, to promote distrust of the forces of law and justice, or to inspire others with a desire to imitate criminals.
- (2) No comics shall explicitly present the unique details and methods of a crime.

- (3) Policemen, judges, Government officials and respected institutions shall never be presented in such a way as to create disrespect for established authority.
- (4) If crime is depicted it shall be as a sordid and unpleasant activity.
- (5) Criminals shall not be presented so as to be rendered glamorous or to occupy a position which creates a desire for emulation.
- (6) In every instance good shall triumph over evil and the criminal punished for his misdeeds.
- (7) Scenes of excessive violence shall be prohibited. Scenes of brutal torture, excessive and unnecessary knife and gunplay, physical agony, gory and gruesome crime shall be eliminated.
- (8) No unique or unusual methods of concealing weapons shall be shown.
- (9) Instances of law-enforcement officers dying as a result of a criminal's activities should be discouraged.
- (10) The crime of kidnapping shall never be portrayed in any detail, nor shall any profit accrue to the abductor or kidnaper. The criminal or the kidnaper must be punished in every case.
- (11) The letters of the word "crime" on a comics-magazine cover shall never be appreciably greater in dimension than the other words contained in the title. The word "crime" shall never appear alone on a cover.
- (12) Restraint in the use of the word "crime" in titles or subtitles shall be exercised.

General standards—Part B
- (1) No comic magazine shall use the word horror or terror in its title.
- (2) All scenes of horror, excessive bloodshed, gory or gruesome crimes, depravity, lust, sadism, masochism shall not be permitted.
- (3) All lurid, unsavory, gruesome illustrations shall be eliminated.
- (4) Inclusion of stories dealing with evil shall be used or shall be published only where the intent is to illustrate a moral issue and in no case shall evil be presented alluringly, nor so as to injure the sensibilities of the reader.
- (5) Scenes dealing with, or instruments associated with walking dead, torture, vampires and vampirism, ghouls, cannibalism, and werewolfism are prohibited.

General standards—Part C
All elements or techniques not specifically mentioned herein, but which are contrary to the spirit and intent of the code, and are considered violations of good taste or decency, shall be prohibited.

Dialogue
- (1) Profanity, obscenity, smut, vulgarity, or words or symbols which have acquired undesirable meanings are forbidden.
- (2) Special precautions to avoid references to physical afflictions or deformities shall be taken.
- (3) Although slang and colloquialisms are acceptable, excessive use should be discouraged and, wherever possible, good grammar shall be employed.

Religion
- (1) Ridicule or attack on any religious or racial group is never permissible.

Costume
- (1) Nudity in any form is prohibited, as is indecent or undue exposure.
- (2) Suggestive and salacious illustration or suggestive posture is

unacceptable.
- (3) All characters shall be depicted in dress reasonably acceptable to society.
- (4) Females shall be drawn realistically without exaggeration of any physical qualities. NOTE.—It should be recognized that all prohibitions dealing with costume, dialog, or artwork applies as specifically to the cover of a comic magazine as they do to the contents.

Marriage and sex
- (1) Divorce shall not be treated humorously nor represented as desirable.
- (2) Illicit sex relations are neither to be hinted at nor portrayed. Violent love scenes as well as sexual abnormalities are unacceptable.
- (3) Respect for parents, the moral code, and for honorable behavior shall be fostered. A sympathetic understanding of the problems of love is not a license for morbid distortion.
- (4) The treatment of live-romance stories shall emphasize the value of the home and the sanctity of marriage.
- (5) Passion or romantic interest shall never be treated in such a way as to stimulate the lower and baser emotions.
- (6) Seduction and rape shall never be shown or suggested.
- (7) Sex perversion or any inference to same is strictly forbidden.

CODE FOR ADVERTISING MATTER

These regulations are applicable to all magazines published by members of the Comics Magazine Association of America, Inc. Good taste shall be the guiding principle in the acceptance of advertising.
- (1) Liquor and tobacco advertising is not acceptable.
- (2) Advertisement of sex or sex instruction books are unacceptable.
- (3) The sale of picture postcards, "pinups," "art studies," or any other reproduction of nude or seminude figures is prohibited.
- (4) Advertising for the sale of knives or realistic gun facsimiles is prohibited.
- (5) Advertising for the sale of fireworks is prohibited.
- (6) Advertising dealing with the sale of gambling equipment or printed matter dealing with gambling shall not be accepted.
- (7) Nudity with meretricious purpose and salacious postures shall not be permitted in the advertising of any product; clothed figures shall never be presented in such a way as to be offensive or contrary to good taste or morals.
- (8) To the best of his ability, each publisher shall ascertain that all statements made in advertisements conform to fact and avoid misrepresentation.
- (9) Advertisement of medical, health, or toiletry products of questionable nature are to be rejected. Advertisements for medical, health, or toiletry products endorsed by the American Medical Association, or the American Dental Association, shall be deemed acceptable if they conform with all other conditions of the Advertising Code.[1]

---

1 "The Comics Code of 1954." *Comic Book Legal Defense Fund*, http://cbldf.org/the-comics-code-of-1954/.

THE RUBBER THAT RUBS YOU OUT
25 YEARS LATER, THE SATIRICAL GERMAN COMIC BOOK ADAPTATION KILLER CONDOM IS A SUBVERSIVE CLASSIC IN NEED OF ITS CULT

BY JUSTIN CHANNELL

In the early days of DVD, Trey Parker's college-era film debut *Cannibal! The Musical* was a staple for fans of *South Park* and cult movies. At a time when DVD buyers lauded releases for the quality and quantity of their bonus features, the *Cannibal!* disc became infamous for its bonus features, most notably a raucous drunken commentary. However, the most curious of videophiles also discovered a wealth of self-promotional material from the film's distributor, Troma Entertainment. An early adopter of the format, Troma saw the marketing power of bonus features and loaded its DVDs with trailers and clips from its vast catalog of B-movies and new lo-fi material videotaped at the company's Hell's Kitchen headquarters. As a result, many hardcore *South Park* fanatics were first introduced to the gutter-humored, penny-pinching stylings of one of America's oldest and strangest exploitation film distributors.

One of the trailers included on the disc was for a film titled *Killer Condom*. Despite the title providing all of the description necessary to draw in Troma's typical B-movie crowd, the trailer narration further explained the story: A hardened NYC detective named Luigi Mackeroni is investigating a series of violent genital mutilations attributed to living contraceptives, only to discover a shocking conspiracy that only he can stop.

The deadpan narrator presents the concept as a serious sci-fi thriller, but it doesn't seem believable until he namedrops legendary artist H.R. Giger. How could the Academy Award-winning creator of the terrifying xenomorph from *Alien*, an artist

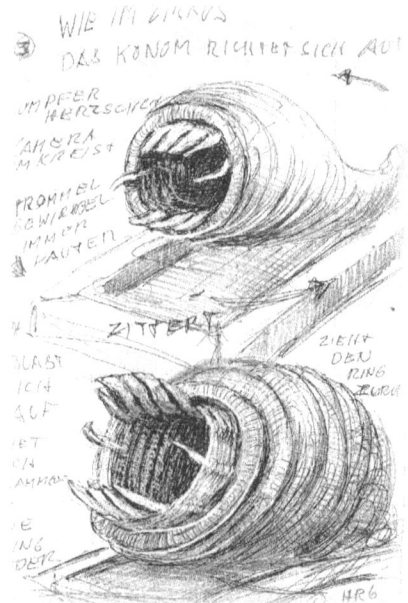

This sketch of the monster condom from the climax of Kondom des Grauens bears similarities to Giger's work on Alejandro Jodorowsky's aborted Dune adaptation. (Photo courtesy of Martin Walz). All Rights Reserved.

famed for his distinctively disturbing airbrush stylings, have contributed to a midnight movie about sentient prophylactics with razor-sharp teeth?

All of this strangeness, plus the repetition of the tagline, "The Rubber That Rubs You Out," was enough to seal the deal for young *South Park* fans looking for a goofy scatological laugh.

But those who sought the film found quite the bait and switch, as is typical of many a Troma title. Instead of being a sci-fi horror film with a scatological bent, as promised in the trailer, *Killer Condom* is a stylish satire tackling multiple struggles faced by the gay community. Although it's set in New York City, the German production keeps the dialogue in its mother tongue, reversing a trope usually seen in Hollywood. After all, think of how many American-produced films make their European characters speak English for the audience's convenience.

With production values that far exceed the typical schlock film and themes that run far deeper than the low-brow expectations set by its salacious title, *Killer Condom* is a unique and intriguing production that delivers on its promises, while simultaneously subverting expectations. It's a true gem among the Troma library, although it has struggled to find an audience despite Troma's best promotional efforts.

However, one has only to speak with principal members of the film's creative team to learn that the final product was a disappointment to everyone involved, especially Ralf König, the creator of the underground comic books upon which the film was based.

While the degree of disappointment varies among those interviewed, one fact is very clear: The film's full potential and success was compromised by a variety of factors. Yet, despite the hurdles, soured relationships among the creative minds, and film's low box office turnout, *Killer Condom* remains a fascinating film that is still in search of its cult.

Opening the Wrapper

Throughout the 1980s, cartoonist Ralf König went from creating underground comic strips in gay magazines to finding mainstream success in Germany with his graphic novels *Der bewegte Mann* (translation: *The Most Desirable Man*) and *Kondom des Grauens* (directly translated as *Condom of Fear*, but later translated to English as *Killer Condom*), both released in 1987. These comics dealt with serious gay themes through a heightened cartoon style that managed to appeal to mainstream Deutsch heterosexual readers as well.

The cross-appeal of König's work caught the eye of artists in other mediums. Film director Martin Walz approached König about making a film adaption of *Der bewegte Mann* but struggled to find financing.

"I couldn't pull it off," Walz recalled in 2020. "I couldn't get it financed, although it was later made with the same lead actor I wanted to have, by a company I tried to get it financed by. Although, in fairness, people did try before me, so I wasn't the first one."

The film adaptation of *Der bewegte Mann*, eventually released in 1994, was a resounding success. At the time, it was the highest-grossing German-produced film released in the country. Orion Classics retitled it *Maybe…Maybe Not* for a theatrical and VHS release in the U.S., a title that carried over to the later U.S. translation of the source material.

The success of *Der bewegte Mann* made Walz reconsider an adaptation of König's work. Revisiting König's catalogue, Walz decided that the story *Kondom des Grauens*—and its sequel, *Bis auf die Knochen* (*Down to the Bone*)—made for a more interesting film.

Parodies of Western horror films and crime noir, the two comics centered on a hard-boiled gay detective with a very realistic Italian name—Luigi Mackeroni—and his

From left, Peter Lohrmeyer and Udo Samel in Kondom des Grauens (Publicity still courtesy of Ascot Elite/Troma)

run-ins with the titular murderous prophylactics. The first book covers Luigi being assigned the outlandish case because of his homosexual lifestyle, shown through his relationship with a young prostitute named Billy. But the case becomes personal when Luigi's legendary manhood and sexual prowess is almost cut short after one of the condoms takes one of his testicles.

Bis auf die Knochen finds Luigi on another strange case: Gay men are turning up dead, with only their skeletons intact. This time, a heterosexual partner joins Luigi to solve the case. The condoms make a comeback in the sequel, and Luigi tracks their origins to a biochemical compound where the local Professor Smirnoff has been working. As he gets closer, however, Luigi discovers Smirnoff is actually a pawn of Dr. Doris Riffleson, an insane Christian doctor using Smirnoff's work to create condoms that will punish sinners and perverts before Jesus Christ returns to cast judgement on humanity.

While the plots of *Kondom des Grauens* and *Bis auf die Knochen* are certainly more outlandish than *Der bewegte Mann*, Walz found it much easier to find financing to produce *Kondom des Grauens* as a film, largely thanks to producers' desire to mine more box office gold from König's popularity.

"I had a crazy producer in Berlin, and we came up with the tagline in three languages, and he sent it out, and somebody bid," said Walz. "It was completely financed privately, which is pretty uncommon here."

The private financing came from Ascot Elite Entertainment Group, a Swiss company infamous for producing sexploitation films and Jess Franco pictures like *Jack the Ripper* and *Swedish Nympho Slaves*. Company founder and former director Erwin C. Dietrich served as a producer alongside his children, Ralph and Karin. Although Ascot's productions had declined since the heyday of the 1970s, the company's distribution arm was still strong throughout Switzerland and Germany in the 1990s, handling high-profile releases like *Evita* and *Dead Man Walking*. In fact, it remains strong in 2021.

Providing a budget of 5.5 million German marks, Ascot expected a success on par with *Der bewegte Mann*. In a 2021 email correspondence, Ralph S. Dietrich confirmed that the success of the prior König adaptation served as a primary motivation for the production of *Kondom des Grauens*.

"There was a huge hype around Ralf König and *Der bewegte Mann*," Dietrich said. "This was the driving force for *Kondom des Grauens*. Ralf was not so satisfied with the outcome of *Der bewegte Mann* and therefore wanted more influence on his next film. He was on the set every day and also had approval of cast, etc. We did everything according to his gusto."

König collaborated with Walz and consultant Mario Kramp on the screenplay. Speaking through a translator via email in 2020, König noted that adapting his comic books to a screenplay was an easy process.

"I remember that everything went pretty quickly with the script and that there were few complaints," König wrote.

Walz echoed König's fond memory of the collaboration, though he did admit that there was some resentment from his collaborators after the final edit of the film. "They were pretty mad at me too, because we edited out a subplot they were pretty fond of," Walz said.

The film's plot combines the two comic books to an extent, largely ignoring the core story of *Bis auf die Knochen* but retaining the ending with Dr. Riffleson and Professor Smirnoff. While Luigi and Billy's relationship is explored, we also get insight into Luigi's past romantic flings with the new character Babette. When they met, Babette was Bob—Luigi's partner—but she discovered her true gender after they shared a night of passionate sex. While she remains obsessed with Luigi, he is more interested in his young fling.

However, more new story aspects are explored, including a scene that drives home the killer condoms' representation of the AIDS epidemic. Early in the film, the police department treat the condoms as a joke, as the only victims are people whom the police consider to be perverts living on the dredges of society. However, when presidential candidate Dick McGouvern is attacked by one of the condoms while bathing with his mistress, the police quickly take notice. As it was with the AIDS epidemic, the killer condoms are only a problem when straight people are in danger.

It's no surprise that König found the adaptation process easy. In the source material, the story is presented like a movie in print form, with the cover bearing the subtitle "ein kollennasen horrorfilm" ("a colossal horror film") and the book beginning

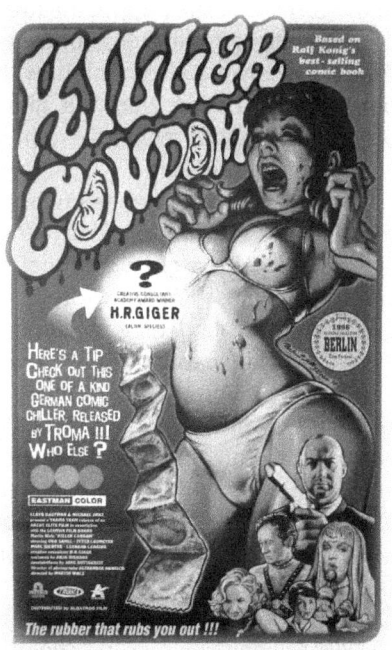

The artwork for the Japanese release of Killer Condom. *Image courtesy Martin Walz.*

with printed opening credits, complete with a "A Film by Ralf König" title card. *Kondom des Grauens* was always destined for the screen to some degree.

"I think cinematically even when I'm drawing comics, and the comics were already a kind of storyboard in that sense," König wrote. "I think, at first, I just typed up the finished speech bubbles and then tried to craft the two stories into a bit of a whole and give the characters more weight here and there. Before the film, there was a *Killer Condom* puppet theatre that ran with great success on stage. Babette, for example, already played a role there, but she doesn't appear in the comic. So, the script was made up of the comic and the puppet theatre."

Regardless, the producers' expectations were clearly high, with both writers noting that the film's preproduction and release were met with much enthusiasm.

"Everyone on the team was completely convinced that this was going to be a great and mega-successful film," König wrote. He then noted with a degree of caution, "That's always a warning sign!"

"It was a pretty big movie in Germany at the time," said Walz. "I was pretty mad that we didn't get any nominations for the German film awards back then, especially for art direction, camera, and lead actor. They just snubbed us."

Walz chuckled at the sentiment of *Killer Condom* winning prestigious awards, but he has a point. The film boasts impressive production value for a premise destined for a smaller cult film market, which also speaks to the faith producers had in König's name value.

"The film that was in my head, that I was hoping for this to look like, was *Little Shop of Horrors*, the remake," Walz said of the visual style.

Viewers can easily see the crew's effort to make a film on par with what Frank Oz accomplished with the *Little Shop* remake. The sets of the film bear a sense of heightened reality that lends to the off-kilter comic book tone permeating the feature. For a European film that takes place in New York City—one of the most cinematically recognizable American cities—the sets never quite manage

The German crew of Kondom des Grauens shoot on the exterior set of the Hotel Quickie, made to appear like New York City in this shot from the movie magazine." (Courtesy Martin Walz. All Rights Reserved)

to convey an accurate portrayal. Though, much like the subversion of a German-speaking cast in an American-set film, the mixture of sets and on-location footage never leads the audience to question where the action takes place, even if the production methods are obvious.

However, the sets—and their obvious shortcomings—were one of the aspects that König saw as a warning sign.

"It was supposed to be set in New York, but you could always tell it was very German," he wrote. "The sets were theatrical. The hotel was made of plywood walls, which you can see."

König certainly has a point. The hotel sets do have a certain rough quality, and Walz even admits on the DVD commentary that the exterior set was constructed in a backyard in Berlin. However, the sets feel fitting for both the film's intended visual style and the rough-hewn locale of a sleazy hourly rate hotel in New York City.

Interestingly, some of the film's set choices can be attributed to the production designer, Agi Ariunsaichan Dawaachu, a Mongolian man who got his start in the industry on *Killer Condom*. In the commentary, Walz explains that Dawaachu did not know what New York City looked like when he took the job. Walz recalled that the production sent Dawaachu on a trip to the Big Apple for research after he built art deco-inspired sets. He returned to say, "You could have mentioned it looked like Moscow."

Walz later noted in 2020 that many of the sets only finished for what appears in the actual frame. He explains, for example, in "lots of shots in the hospital…the paint stopped two inches outside of the frame."

Killer Condom also boasts an impressive cast of German stars. Udo Samel, who, at the time, was known to German-speaking audiences for his dramatic leading roles in *Kaspar Hauser* and Wim Winders's *Faraway, So Close!*, stepped into the role of Luigi Mackeroni. Walz said that Samel's agent was nervous about the decision, admitting that it "wasn't the wisest career move."

Peter Lohmeyer, Samel's costar in *Kaspar Hauser*, was cast as Mackeroni's partner, Sam, in another holdover from *Bis auf die Knochen*. The villainous Dr. Doris Riffleson was portrayed by Iris Berben, an actress with a long career in film and television, who was then just launching her iconic TV series *Rosa Roth*.

In addition, Leonard Lansink, who appeared in *Der bewegte Mann* as a character in drag, donned women's clothing once again to play Babette. Lansink would later go on to play the private detective on the popular TV series *Wilsberg*, which is still airing new episodes as of 2021.

Many other German film and TV stars appear in the cast in bit parts, and in the commentary, Walz said that others later asked why they hadn't been asked to be involved.

Apart from the cast, another impressive aspect of the film is its special effects, which were not created by a professional FX team, but instead by a crew of creative young artists with more experience in experimentation than perfection.

"More Like Experimenting"

Jörg Buttgereit wasn't used to

being a work-for-hire artist.

As the director of the gory underground art films *Nekromantik*, *Der Todesking*, and *Schramm*, Buttgereit has a style of filmmaking that more closely resembles auteur theory than a trade. While working on his independent films, he would take on countless jobs, including directing, editing, and special effects. He never expected to be a professional special-effects artist when Walz approached him with the job.

"If I would have been in his position, I wouldn't hire me," Buttgereit recalled, "because I couldn't tell him all the solutions he was looking for. It was more like experimenting with stuff. To me, it was kind of unprofessional how they hired us, because we had no experience with mainstream."

The "unprofessional" way Buttgereit landed the job of bringing killer condoms to life was a referral from Beatrice Manowski, the lead actress from *Nekromantik*. Manowski was dating Walz at the time, and Walz thought Buttgereit and his team were perfect to take on the challenge of making carnivorous condoms come to life for the first time in cinema.

"He saw all my movies…and they were looking for someone who could shoot all the special-effects scenes—because he hated to do that—on a decent budget. But this so-called decent budget for me was a big budget. So, I actually hired lots of my friends, like Daktari Lorenz, the main actor from *Nekromantik*. He did most of the special effects for that movie.

"They hired me for a fixed price,

This image and p. 71: The giant killer condom prop created by Jörg Buttgereit's effects team as it appears in 2021. The prop is currently held in the private collection of Ascot Elite's head of sales and distribution, Roman Güttinger." Photo Courtesy and copyright Jörg Buttgereit. All rights reserved.

and they also hired my crew. When we needed stuff, they just gave it to us. I didn't have to do the production of the second unit. So, that was really, for my standards, a big budget, because I had no budget before that, and now I had things like catering, and I could pay the friends, or they paid the friends.

"And the only reason they hired me was because I knew the girlfriend of the director, and he kind of convinced me... because I told him, I don't know how we could animate those little condom things."

Despite Buttgereit's initial apprehension, Walz remains confident in his decision to this day, still impressed by the work done by the scrappy crew, especially on the first day of shooting.

"The producer in Berlin was a con artist," said Walz. "I didn't trust any of these people, and that's why we started with a very high-class sequence."

The sequence involves Luigi using video surveillance on rooms at the Hotel Quickie. He mistakenly interrupts Babette entertaining a john, only to find their condom is not of the carnivorous variety. But one of the killer condoms does strike in another room and leads Luigi on an elaborate chase through the sex hotel.

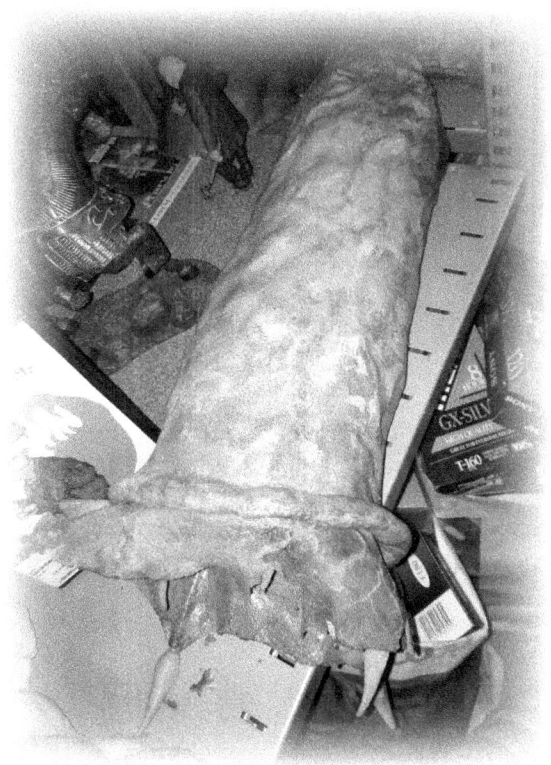

"We figured if we do really well the first two days of shooting and edit it right away, they're going to leave us the fuck alone after that, which is exactly what happened," Walz remembered. "They were quite impressed. It was a head start really."

Any of Buttgereit's concerns of not being a professional effects artist were squashed when the time came to shoot the first effect of the sequence: a prostitute screaming while holding the killer condom— complete with her john's severed penis—which then jumps out of her hand. The entire effects sequence was all completed in one take.

"I don't actually know how Jörg and all these people did it!" Walz excitedly recalled about the sequence.

"But it was actually one take, and it jumped out of her hand and scurried on the floor and down the hallway, and at the end, it disappeared, but the dick is still there."

Unfortunately, the sequence is nowhere to be found in any released version of the film. Walz and Buttgereit recalled that during postproduction, the producers decided they would have better luck making their money back with a lower (more accessible) rating. As a result, much of the gore that Buttgereit and his crew created either wound up on the cutting-room floor or was never filmed at all in order to get the German classification equivalent of a PG-13 rating in the U.S.

Buttgereit created the condoms and brought them to life through traditional special-effects methods. Obviously, real condoms being made of latex made choosing the material for the monsters quite easy. For various movements, Buttgereit's crew built larger sets and used other classic practical-effects tricks.

"We made the condoms [oversized], and we built little pieces of the set at a bigger size," Buttgereit explained. "That way, we could use hand puppets of the killer condoms, and it was all just a little bit bigger than it was on the screen. And we all did it in the studio. So, we always had to refer to the original footage and try to make it.

"We shot more footage—really disgusting footage. We shot footage when the condoms bite off the dick of someone. We also shot, like, when the condom is vomiting the dick out again. The producer said, 'No, that's too gross.'

"The sad thing is that they never really used the strong footage we gave to them, so there never was a director's cut or anything, because it was during the editing that they decided we had to go to 16 certification to make the money back. So, all the film clips with the strong footage we did…they're kind of lost. I might have some photographs, but the film footage…I don't know if it exists at this point."

While the thought of a PG-13 film in the U.S. featuring severed genitalia heavily in the plot sounds absurd, Walz pointed out that much of the editing may not have even been necessary.

"It got a 16 rating in Germany, so I have no idea why they edited it out, because we're not that prudish with sex, so I'm pretty sure we would've gotten the 16 rating anyway," Walz said.

Unfortunately, these cuts were done quickly, and because the audio mix had to remain intact, they resulted in some awkward editing. Walz is not happy with the changes to these sequences, as he would have preferred to tighten up other parts of the film.

"They should've given us another few weeks to reconsider shit, because the second half is struggling a little bit."

Time was always a factor on the set of *Killer Condom*. According to Walz, "It was a very strict schedule. It was 14-hour days, and we were editing at the same time, so Sunday was in the editing room. It went on for 42 days."

The long shooting schedule was also a factor in souring König's idea of the film's potential. König noted that the long working hours left everyone "quickly exhausted."

Buttgereit also grew despondent from the restrictions placed on the production. Coming from a background of underground filmmaking that required him to have a hand in many aspects of the craft, his effects work on *Killer Condom* did not quite satisfy his artistic interests.

"I was just producing the stuff, giving it away, getting paid for it… very unromantic…very unusual for me, because I was used to this artist approach where I do everything on my movie and have total control," Buttgereit said. "So, that was kind of frustrating."

Walz has his own regrets about what could have been, especially regarding the extreme shooting schedule, saying, "I don't think I would ever do anything like that again."

While the disappointment in the final product varies between König, Walz, and Buttgereit, they all do agree on one thing: The producers wasted the talent of their most valuable creative member—someone who had major international name value.

Giger, "Creative Consultant"

The "creative consultant" credit given H.R. Giger is usually met with surprise by anyone discovering *Killer Condom*. After all, despite the sexual, often phallic nature of Giger's work, it seems surprising that an Oscar-winning effects artist would work on an international film with a concept so lewd that only Troma would handle U.S. distribution.

However, *Killer Condom* was

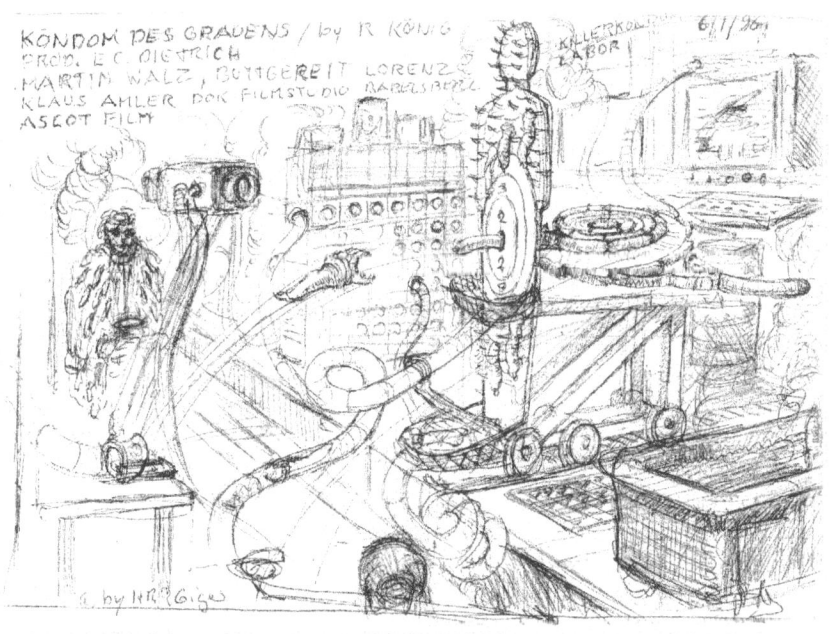

According to director Martin Walz, H.R. Giger was especially pleased the production used this design of a training ground for killer condoms. (Photo courtesy of Martin Walz. All Rights Reserved)

financed by a team in Giger's native Switzerland, and the team was aware that his name and association were valuable. Involving Giger in the film—especially a film with sci-fi elements—could further boost the team's aspirations of box office success. Everyone involved was interested in having an artist of Giger's stature on board.

"[Giger] had a lot of fun with the idea of biting condoms," König wrote. "He was even obsessed with it! But the producers didn't really take the man seriously (as they didn't take him seriously in Switzerland for a long time, anyway); they just wanted his name on the poster as a 'creative consultant.'"

Giger was not involved at the start of the film. As Buttgereit and Walz recalled, contract negotiations occurred during production. In fact, Buttgereit was already creating and filming the titular effects shots when he learned from producer Ralph S. Dietrich that Giger was coming aboard.

"I was a big fan of him, like everybody, and that was exciting," Buttgereit said. "We didn't really work together, but we were corresponding a lot. Because he got his contract so late, our work was mostly finished. But he came over and he visited us, and we spent time going to eat sushi, and I visited him in his own private museum in Switzerland. So, we became kind of connected. Giger watched my films and he liked them a lot. Even if he couldn't really put much work in the movie, I think he's called a 'creative consultant.' It really means we had dinner with him and watched movies."

However, Walz noted that some of Giger's work did appear in the film. In fact, all of the principals interviewed recall his excitement about the project. They have similar stories of receiving faxes from Giger in the early morning hours, each fax containing concepts for *Kondom des Grauens*. One of the sketches referenced by the crew was of a giant killer condom that Dr. Riffleson created specifically to attack Luigi's mammoth member during the film's climax. When viewed today, the sketch bears a strong resemblance to the work Giger did for Alejandro Jodorowksy's failed adaptation of *Dune*.

"He did much more than design a condom, and he did not design the small condoms," Walz said, noting Buttgereit's work earlier in production.

Indeed, the sketches that Walz shared from the archive of Giger art created for *Kondom des Grauens* show the artist's vision for the film's final set piece: an underground laboratory hidden in a church where a kidnapped scientist creates living, evil condoms for a right-wing zealot. Giger's designs for the laboratory, which appear in the final film, include characters dangling on swings above a pool of killer condoms, as well as a training ground for budding condoms. One aspect of his original sketch of the swings that did not appear is a set of Olympic rings, which, according to Walz, reflected Giger's distaste for the Olympics. Even the secret entrance to the lab within the church set was sketched out by Giger as a simple crucifix on a podium; when shifted, the crucifix revealed a secret entrance. Walz even remembers adding details to the laboratory set, minutiae Giger had suggested that were not connected to the film's narrative in any way.

"One of his favorite things was this castration machine that we put in there even though it had nothing to do with the movie," Walz said of Giger.

Despite Giger's designs appearing only in the final act of the film, Walz was grateful to receive kind words about the film from Giger following the premiere—which was, unfortunately, a bit disastrous thanks to inclement weather.

"He wrote a very nice letter to me after the film came out," said Walz. "We had the worst opening ever, because they were all open-air, and it was always raining. The big opening was in Zurich, where the distribution company was. It was at a lake with a huge screen, and it was pissing. You couldn't hear the dialogue.

"We had another one in Cologne, and it was raining there as well. But Giger was there, and he saw it and wrote a very nice letter about it. I keep hearing that he was bitching about all of his movies, so, at least to me, he was glad about this one."

Despite the negative feelings König harbors for the final film, the chance to meet with the legendary artist was a positive mark.

"The best thing about the film was that I was allowed to visit H.R. Giger personally in Zurich…and got to know him," König wrote.

Producers wanted to film the meeting between the two artists as a promotional "making of" documentary, but König refused, preferring to keep the encounter private.

"Giger was genius and madness in person! He had a self-built 'ghost train' in his Zurich row house, in the garden, in the Giger style, with which we had to turn immediately…before the man greeted us properly at all! The whole house was stuffed with Giger art, the famous paintings, painted skulls, the Oscar for *Alien*—everything was lying around, chaotic and dusty…like the gloomy cave of a mad wizard."

Making New York 'Look Fake Too'

While the production team did its best to make the German sets look like New York City, the producers knew there was nothing quite as convincing as showing the real location on screen. Any attempt at tricking an international audience—especially a U.S. audience—would require exterior shots of the Big Apple's many landmarks. The Dietrichs sent Walz, a skeleton crew, and some key cast members to New York and filled in the crew gaps with locals in the city.

"We were running around New York City with a documentary crew, basically…like, five people," Walz recalled.

The guerilla shoot required Walz and company to be quick, disobey rules, and use their status as a foreign crew to their advantage. It also required them to gain the trust of the American crew.

Walz and the other Germans soon noticed that the American crew, consisting mostly of film students who aspired to direct, began questioning decisions and offering personal input. According to Walz, he and his crew eventually had to prove themselves with a stylish trick during one of the exterior shots featuring Samel and Lohmeyer.

"We put the actors in the shadow and had the sun start right behind them," Walz said in the commentary, "and it makes the shot look like a back-projection, but then you're really surprised when Udo Samel turns around and walks into the 'screen.' The problem was that we had shot already in Berlin all the studio stuff—which, of course, looked kind of fake—and now we were coming to New York and had to make New York look fake too.

"It took some ideas, but I think it looked pretty fine. You don't really feel the transitions too much."

Remembering the same moment in 2020, Walz said, "That's when the American crew realized, 'Oh, they want something different. They know what they're doing.'"

Buttgereit agreed in the DVD commentary, noting that the crew members who didn't travel to New York City—most of the crew—were impressed by the results, although he admits that "if you're watching it in New York, you're not too impressed, but, for us, it was something big."

König feels the opposite, writing, "Kind of disturbing are the short exterior shots, which really did take place in New York just to have Mackeroni walk the streets for a change. I would have been really consistent trash and shot it in Frankfurt, between the skyscrapers, but claimed that was New York."

Dealing with permits and regulations while working on a low-budget shoot in a major city can be difficult, but Walz was familiar enough with New York City to know that many of the shots they needed would be possible with a bit of creative maneuvering. During the shoot, Walz was informed by the local production manager that the crew would be unable to get shots from a camera coming up out of a manhole in Times Square, nor would they be able to shoot the exterior of a police station or Luigi smoking his trademark cigarette on the subway.

All of the aforementioned shots appear in the film—and they were all shot on location in New York City.

The only regret Walz says he has from the shoot is the manhole shot, saying that he "should have given a little light into the hole so you understand that we're going underground." As that shot appears in the film, the lighting is a bit too dark, so it just appears like the camera is moving up from street level. Regardless, pushback from the organizers forced Walz to take matters into his own hands to get the shot at all.

"I said, 'There are, like, 280

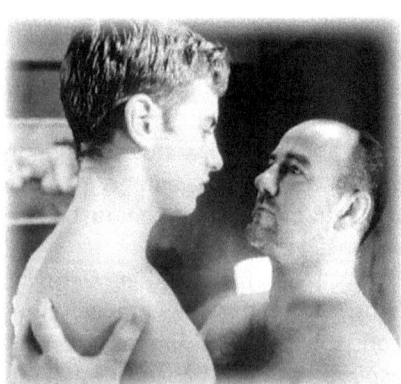

Marc Richter and Udo Samel as Billy and Luigi in Kondom des Grauens (Publicity still courtesy of Ascot Elite/Troma. All Rights Reserved)

manholes in Times Square; we gotta find one that opens.' They kept saying, 'No, no, no,' but at one point, somebody got into it and found something…and the same thing too with 'You're not allowed to shoot a police station in New York City.'"

Walz solved the police station problem by having his American organizer and Bavarian director of photography approach officers at the station, both pretending to be members of a documentary crew needing a shot of the building. The DOP laid on a thick amount of gracious praise for the American police and the kindness of Americans, which Walz said was key to getting permission for the shot.

"The police guy just said, 'OK, get the fuck out of here; go get your shot and piss off.' So, we got all these things done that were supposed to be not legal or not possible, and some stuff we just went in and shot."

The shots of Luigi smoking in the subway and getting out of a taxi in the final pre-Giuliani days of Times Square were no different. Walz and the crew simply filmed Samel in the real locations and left as soon as possible. Samel was excited to film in Times Square, but on the commentary track, Walz recalled that the scene was filmed in such a guerilla, run-and-gun fashion that the final shot in the film includes a real commuter trying to get a ride from the production cab.

"I knew the city, so I wasn't falling for a lot of shit where they said we couldn't do that. I said, 'We'll figure it out. We'll make it possible somehow.'"

Walz did manage to find out how to get all of the New York City exterior shots needed for *Killer Condom*, including an impressive crane shot to end the film. It would not be the last time the film traveled to the city.

'A Huge Start'

Ascot first released *Kondom des Grauens* in August 1996 in Switzerland, Austria, and Germany—countries where the company's expectations were highest. As the Dietrichs were expecting to match the box office gross of *Der bewegte Mann*, they embarked on what Walz called "a huge launch" for the film. Bearing their coveted 16 certification and with mainstream dollar signs in their eyes, the Dietrichs launched a marketing campaign for the film that included a full-color magazine and a soundtrack released via Polygram Records—complete with a techno theme song. Walz noted on the DVD commentary that rap and hip-hop acts were originally courted, but they all turned the gig down due to the film's homosexual content.

However, Walz said that Ascot never completed its plans to market the film, and he felt this was a detriment to initial efforts. The marketing campaign would have first featured the then-familiar König drawing of Luigi Mackeroni, followed by a second set of ads showing the drawing side by side with a photo of Samel. Finally, there would have been posters promoting the live-action elements only. Ascot used only König's drawing of Luigi as key art, a decision that Walz believes hurt the film's performance.

"It was a huge start, because the company thought they were going to beat *Maybe…Maybe Not*, which had, maybe, 3 million plus attendance or something, and we ended up with, like, half a million. Reviews were mixed. It got a huge start, but they didn't do much advertising for it in the end. They never did what they promised to do.

"It was not bad for a movie like this, but [it was] not what they expected."

While the marketing of the film was not to Walz's liking, a copy of the magazine he provided does show a merchandising push focusing on König's characters and comic books. König's comic book artwork is offered in mail-in ads throughout the periodical on everything, including CD-ROM screensavers, key chains, cigarette lighters—even a mug. Whether you started your day with a cigarette, a cup of coffee, or both, you could get a look at Luigi Mackeroni's cartoon genitals peeking out of a bathrobe. Then, as you head to work, you could take a 3-D replica of Germany's most well-endowed detective with you on your key chain!

The magazine shows an incredible amount of optimism, with features on all of the actors and the principals of the crew. Many of Giger's sketches, as well as photos of Buttgereit's effects—some of which had already hit the cutting-room floor—were printed alongside comparisons featuring König's artwork.

While the reviews of the film were mixed, the harshest critic was König himself. He still hasn't watched the film since catching it on VHS, and he was too embarrassed to attend the premiere.

"I thought the film was really very bad. The audience thought so too; they were quickly out of the cinemas. The film is boring—no pace, no timing. I didn't think it was possible with this crazy material!

"That's why I was very optimistic about everything during the shoot. I could see that some things weren't going well, but I was reassured that once there was sound on it and the film was edited, everything would be great. But what looks like crap during filming looks like crap later on the screen; that's what I learned. The well-known actors realized already during the shooting that they might have made a mistake, because the work on the film was very unprofessional. Fees were not paid on time; shooting time was far too short; the team consisted almost entirely of beginners from film schools, who brought a lot of enthusiasm but had no idea how to solve problems. The producers made everything worse, and there was a lot of appeasement and lying. Martin

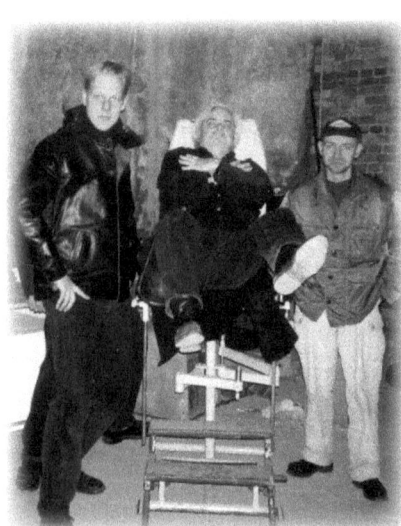

From left, Jörg Buttgereit, H.R. Giger, and Daktari Lorenz on the set of Kondom des Grauens. (Photo courtesy of Jörg Buttgereit. All Rights Reserved.)

Walz wanted to make a cool film, but he was also inexperienced and didn't have a handle on things."

However, König does admire the talent of the cast. "Udo Samel would have been a sexy Mackeroni.

"Peter Lohmeyer and Iris Berben are also good, very well-known actors, but also miscast. Jörg Buttgereit is a great guy, very creative. So much would have been possible, but nobody had a plan."

Dietrich recalls that despite König making creative decisions on the film, "at the end, he did not like 'his film' and refused to do PR for it."

Despite König's distancing and the film's financial failure, Dietrich holds a realistic view of the legacy of Kondom des Grauens.

"Well, the film was financially a disaster," he said. "The content was just not mainstream enough; therefore, our budget was way too high. But I'm still proud of this unique film. It was a wild project to begin with. I certainly have very good memories."

Of the memories that Walz has of the film's initial 500-print release across Germany, Switzerland, and Austria is a story of the film's gay content taking an audience by surprise.

"I heard a story where some skinhead fucks were in a cinema in the northern part of Germany, and it took them about half an hour to find out, 'Oh, it's all gay people,'" Walz remembered. "Once they realized—'Oh my god, the only heterosexual people are assholes or maniacs or sidekicks'—they had to leave the cinema."

Post-Tromatic Schlock

Walz said not much happened after the theatrical release of Kondom des Grauens, noting that "the producers were done with it" when the numbers didn't meet their expectations.

Buttgereit added, "Even for Germans, this film is really weird, and I don't think it ever played on TV, just because nobody knows what to do with it."

However, Dietrich said the film did play on television in Germany, noting that it was partially funded by FTV for a prime-time television spot.

Ultimately, however, actor Peter Lohmeyer is the reason why most audiences have seen the film. According to Walz, Lohmeyer was a guest at a German film festival in Los Angeles shortly before production. During the festival, he mentioned that he was appearing in a film called *Killer Condom*, which piqued the curiosity of the selection committee.

"The next year, the American people responsible for the selection…got a big box of German films from the German export, and *Killer Condom* wasn't in there. And they remembered, luckily, and said, 'Where's this condom movie?' So, they handed them the movie, and they put it on. The guy that watched the movie for the first time before they put it in the festival—he called Troma. He knew somebody there and said, 'I've got a movie you're going to want to release.'"

Lloyd Kaufman, the president of Troma Entertainment, believes the person who tipped him off was David Schultz, who, at the time, was working in acquisitions and theatrical for Troma.

"He became a nut about this film," Kaufman said. "He would not stop talking about *Killer Condom*. Finally, I saw the movie, and it was terrific."

Walz recalled that "the movie was two years old when [Troma] took it over, so, basically, dead."

Kaufman agreed, saying, "Unfortunately, the film was not successful, and we bought whatever was left.

"We did our best. The problem was that they spent too much money on it. We lost money on it. It's a great movie, though. I love the film. The idea that they portray New York City as a German-speaking city—it's wonderful."

Despite the financial failure, Kaufman is still very proud of the film, though he feels bitter that the film failed to find its audience.

"It wasn't the film's fault," he said. "We didn't have enough money to promote it properly. People didn't realize it was a mainstream movie, and it had the queer thing going, and it had these shots of prophylactics with teeth, and the name *Killer Condom* didn't help.

"If you pick films that are ahead of their time, you get penalized. People don't show up. We failed with *Killer Condom*, but we're proud of it. And we did have a lot of fun for about 20 years bringing Killer Condom Man to the Cannes Film Festival."

Killer Condom Man was a promotional costumed character that joined the Toxic Avenger, Sgt. Kabukiman N.Y.P.D., Dolphinman, and other colorful characters from Troma-distributed films. Accompanied by scantily clad women and barely bathed volunteers covered in fake blood, Killer Condom Man joined the gang as a regular guest on Cannes' La Croisette from the late '90s until Troma was forced to stop appearing at the festival in 2017.

It's this kind of constant push for *Kondom des Grauens* that left Walz pleased with Troma's handling of the film. He also recalls multiple trips to the U.S. to present it at film festivals.

"They did a really good job in subtitling it. It's a very, very good translation—all the different words that come up for 'penis' and 'condom.' They kinda saved the movie too. If not for Troma, it wouldn't be on the map at all."

Although both Walz and Kaufman recalled Troma owning the world rights to *Kondom des Grauens*, Dietrich noted that Ascot still owns the world rights, excluding Germany; Troma only licensed the film for the U.S. and Canada. According to Dietrich, Troma's licensing has since expired, which appears to be reflected by the film no longer appearing in the film catalogue on the Troma website. However, Dietrich was very pleased with the deal when it was active.

"I only had one meeting with Lloyd," Dietrich said, "a real gentleman. Working with Troma was very pleasant. I can say only the best about Troma."

One strange issue with Troma's handling of the film is that the soundtrack features a drastic change. In a crucial introductory scene, Etta James's "At Last" plays in the German theatrical version. It's during this scene that we are introduced to Babette, who is lip-synching the song on stage. It is also the first time Luigi sees Billy. While the manager of the Hotel Quickie tells Luigi a story, Luigi is distracted by Billy, and "At Last" swells to the point that he no longer hears the manager's inane chatter.

The Troma prints, however, do not feature "At Last." Instead, a remix of Roberta Flack's "Killing Me Softly with His Song" plays, though not the Fugees cover that was popular at the time of the film's release. However, the remix sounds blatantly like the Fugees' version. Small flourishes from the cover version's arrangement are retained, including a Wyclef Jean imitator singing, "One time…two times." But the rest of the modern rap section consists of a Lauren Hill soundalike repeating "1996" over and over again. While Flack's version is also featured in the German version of the film, Walz was taken by surprise when he saw the film's U.S. release for the first time.

The change caused two significant problems in the scene: Babette's lip-synching no longer matches, and the levels of the new mix are not properly adjusted. As a result, the story the hotel manager tells stays at full volume the entire time, while the English subtitles stop.

Kaufman did not recall Troma making any changes to the sound mix and believed the music licensing was completed before Troma involved. Dietrich confirmed that the song was deleted from any releases outside Germany, Austria, and Switzerland due to of the high cost of licensing "At Last" in other territories.

Where the strange Fugees soundalike remix came from is still anyone's guess. Comparisons to multiple remix versions from that time period have turned up no results.

The 25th Anniversary Approaches

With the 25th anniversary of *Kondom des Grauens* approaching in 2021, it seems like there could be some cause for fans to celebrate.

Walz confirmed that Polish film restoration and postproduction company Fixafilm has licensed *Kondom des Grauens* for an eventual Blu-ray release. Fixafilm has scanned Walz's personal print of the film, which contains a few extra scenes. Unfortunately, none of the deleted effects shots was found.

"To my big disappointment, the various dicks…are not included, so they must have been cut out earlier to avoid a higher rating," Walz said. "Such a shame! Especially the first scene with the hooker was such impressive work by Jörg and his team!"

When informed of the film's approaching anniversary, Dietrich noted that he would look into the status of certain elements to consider the possibility of a new transfer of the film. Certainly, this will come as a relief to Walz, who noted many difficulties in obtaining licensing and prints from Ascot in the past.

"I still think it is ridiculous how thoroughly Ascot dropped the film after its release in Germany," Walz said. "It went so far that when some years back, in 2011, the Australian Cinemathèque was looking for a print to screen at their 'Drawn to Screen' program, they were not able to find *one* print anywhere. I ended up sending my long version to Australia. Then, some years later, the DOP, Alex Honisch, found a regular-release print in his attic in Bavaria and sent it to me."

Depending on what elements Dietrich finds—and whether his company chooses to release a new transfer—the two prints Walz mentioned could very well be the last remaining copies of *Kondom des Grauens*.

One issue that modern audiences take with the film involves a scene in which Luigi misgenders Babette by using her birth name, as well as several scenes in which Luigi displays transphobic behavior. Both Walz and König deny that Luigi's transphobia was intentional and maintain that they did not intend any harm by including those scenes.

"I don't remember what exactly is said in the film and what is seen that is supposed to be transphobic by today's standards," König wrote. "It was the '90s; I was often a drag queen myself back then. But maybe we were too insensitive."

Luigi's mistreatment of Babette can also be viewed as a parody of noir detectives turning down their past flames, an interpretation with which Walz agrees.

"He was being a little bit of an asshole," Walz said.

Regardless, casting Leonard Lansink as Babette is another sour moment for Walz, who feels his biggest mistake as the film's director was not listening to a note Lansink provided during casting.

"He was great in casting, but he told me that he was afraid of high heels, and I just ignored him—and I shouldn't have," Walz said. "So, all the fun he had in casting, he never had in the film. I think it was really not a funny part, and it should be a really, really funny part—and he was funny, but he was so focused on not bending his foot that that took up most of his concentration.

"In most of the takes, I could've put him in sneakers. I just didn't. I was busy somewhere else. It was a stupid decision, and it really hurt the actor because he was completely focused on not falling, basically. It's a little bit sour for me on that part."

Walz's regret regarding Lansink's performance outlines another opportunity for perfection that could only be seen in hindsight, one that fueled the disappointment among the creative team behind *Kondom des Grauens*. König prefers his creations to remain as comic books, over which he has full control; Walz laments the changes forced by the producers; Buttgereit wishes his effects hadn't been excised; and Dietrich regrets the financial failure of the film.

However, the film's audience has had a different reaction: *Kondom des Grauens* has gained a reputation as a film that greatly exceeds expectations. Instead of being a low-budget schlock-fest, *Kondom des Grauens* is a biting satire with a great deal of heart. It continues to find an audience around the world, reaching new viewers via streaming platforms (often through blurry, bootleg YouTube uploads of the out-of-print Troma DVD) and recent TV airings in Germany.

While there is no changing the various production issues that disappointed its creators, *Kondom des Grauens* remains a subversive cinematic experience that deserves to find a larger cult following. Here's hoping that if it finds that following in the future, audiences will be able to see it properly restored.

The cast and crew of Kondom des Grauens in happier times in this photo from the movie magazine. (Courtesy Martin Walz)

HOLY SHIT!! MORE KILLER CONDOM GOODNESS!

These storyboards show the scenes of Luigi Mackeroni first discovering the killer condoms and later returning to the scene to blast one out of the air with his service weapon.
(Photo courtesy of Martin Walz)

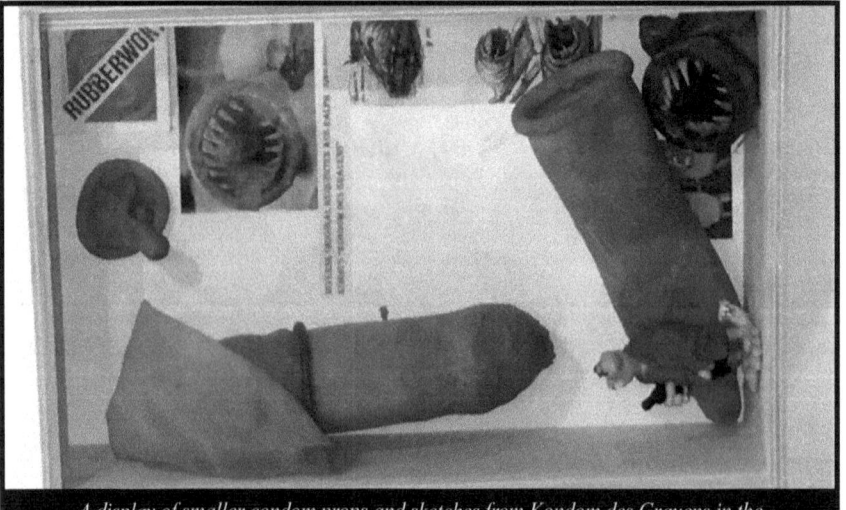

A display of smaller condom props and sketches from Kondom des Grauens in the private collection of Ascot Elite's head of sales and distribution, Roman Güttinger.

EVEN MORE GIGER! (HEY, THEY SENT IT TO US, WE'D BE IDIOTS NOT TO USE THEM!)

This H.R. Giger sketch sent via fax depicts the hidden entrance to the villain's secret lair in Kondom des Grauens. (Photo courtesy of Martin Walz)

Below:
This H.R. Giger sketch of the climatic final scene of Kondom des Grauens appeared in the magazine. Note the Olympic rings in Giger's sketch.

The Olympic rings are notably absent in this set photo. However, some characters have their legs dangling through rings. (Images provided by Martin Walz)

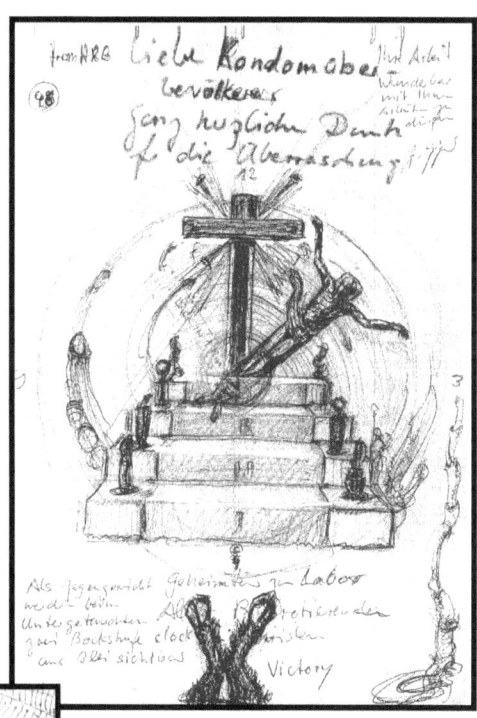

Top:
The cover of Ralf König's comic book Kondom des Grauens.

Middle:
The cover of the Kondom des Grauens movie magazine.

Bottom: This page from the Kondom des Grauens movie magazine shows a variety of merchandise bearing Ralf König's cartoon creation, Luigi Mackeroni.

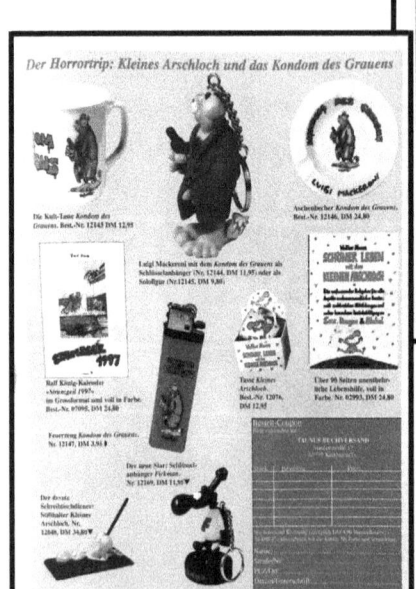

Magazine provided courtesy of Martin Walz.

THE OPEN CENSORSHIP OF PROFESSIONAL WRESTLING OR THE ATTACK OF THE PEACOCK

BY JASON LANE

World Wrestling Entertainment (WWE) has been in the business of entertaining paying audiences for nearly 60 years. Founded in 1963 as the World Wide Wrestling Federation (WWWF), it shortened its title to the World Wrestling Federation (WWF) in '79 and maintained this acronym until 2002, when it became WWE. Hundreds of story angles drew crowds to see heels and villains get their just due at the hands of baby faces and heroes. The action, stories, and results have almost always been predetermined, but that in no way diminishes the hard work—or the pain—that pro-wrestlers put in each time they step into the ring. Just because the action is a work of kayfabe doesn't make the cuts and broken bones any less painful.

Wrestlers' personal sacrifices are there, put on full display, to do one thing and one thing only: to make their employers money. That's just the business.

You can't draw a crowd? Say goodbye. You can't get people to hate you? Say goodbye. You didn't do what we told you? Say goodbye. Did you cause the promoter to lose money? Say double-goodbye. Also, keep in mind, the wrestling business of years past is absolutely nothing like it is now. You have a problem now? Talk to HR, a lawyer, or an agent. You had a legit complaint back then? If you voiced it, you were punished, fired, or blacklisted, as promoters spoke to each other and let others know who was a "troublemaker." Back then, for the sake of your job, you did what you were told. Separate from the more hideous stories some people have told behind the scenes, some of what these people had to do to bring in crowds was horrible. Some of these things took place a very long time ago, while others are disturbingly current. "It was a different time back then" is an applicable saying, but looking at some of these incidents through modern eyes is still shocking. But what are you going to do?

Well, someone just did something.

Not a someone, but a something. Peacock, a streaming service owned by NBCUniversal, gained access to WWE's vast video library. It is a *huge* library. Over the years, WWE purchased many old and/or defunct wrestling companies' video libraries. That, plus WWE's own significant amount of content, makes Peacock, by far, the biggest collection of pro-wrestling on the planet, and it's a definite win for the streaming service.

However....

It was noticed almost immediately after the acquisition that some questionable content had been removed from certain TV episodes from the '80s—an interview here, a threat made there, and some matches missing altogether. Perhaps the biggest match that disappeared totally was Roddy Piper and Bad News Brown's *WrestleMania VI* match. Why was this a match taken out? The feud leading up to the match was heavy with racial overtones, with Bad News Brown portraying an always-angry African American who blamed the system for keeping him down. Piper disagreed vehemently and, to prove that color meant nothing and that "everyone is black and white," painted half his body completely black. Behind the scenes, Bad News Brown was livid, but he went on with the show. Years later, Piper said that he regretted the angle but that his heart was in the right place in trying to show that color wasn't important. Peacock disagreed completely and cut the match entirely.

Another interview, this one from *Survivor Series* 2005, showed Vince McMahon using the N-word, calling John Cena "My n**ga!" WWE reps said it was an attempt to make the McMahon character seem insensitive and out of touch. If that was the goal, they achieved it spectacularly, and Peacock must have agreed, because it cut that scene too.

A few more cuts have been made since, and a *lot* more are on the horizon. This article examines the 30-plus federations comprising WWE's estimated 18,000-plus hours of content, focusing on the most obvious characters, angles, skits, moments, decisions, and reactions likely to be censored by Peacock.

PROBLEMATIC ANGLES

In wrestling, some ideas meant to start or extend feuds begin with the best of greedy intentions, but they can be affected by real-world events, receive too much notice from the "real world," or just be too much to take. The following are some examples.

WWE SmackDown 2005: A young wrestler named Muhammad Hassan (real name Marc Copani) was getting a push as a heel, coming off to the crowd as a (possible) Muslim extremist. Muslim Americans were already voicing their complaints about the character's obvious villainous persona, as well as his practice of extending his arms and giving praise to Allah, which gave the religion a bad look. His speeches described the prejudices and stereotypes created after 9/11, and he blamed the audience for these things as well. A feud began between Hassan and one of the biggest stars in the business, the Undertaker, as a successful run against such an established star would help Hassan go far. A story angle was shot that involved several men in black shirts, camouflaged pants, and black ski masks hitting the Undertaker with clubs and then choking him out with piano wire. The masked men then celebrated by raising Hassan over their heads and carrying him away.

Complaints flooded in immediately, but that was nothing compared to the outrage that occurred three days later, on July 7, 2005, when the London train bombings took place and killed 52 U.K. residents. These suicide attacks drew attention to the wrestling angle (already of questionable taste), which then blew up with the mainstream press, with several major outlets reporting on the subject matter and the complaints from the audience. WWE tried to stymie the flow of negative press, but this strategy did not work in the least. After *SmackDown*'s parent network, UPN, pressured WWE to keep the Hassan character off the network, WWE did so, killing Hassan as a personality. The angle ended at the very next pay-per-view event, the *Great American Bash*, when the Undertaker got his revenge by "injuring" Hassan via a powerbomb (throwing a person onto their flattened back) from the stage ramp to the concrete floor some 10 feet down. The character was said to have been taken to the hospital and sustained massive injuries. The next week, *WWE SmackDown* General Manager Teddy Long stated that because of Hassan's injuries, he would no longer be allowed to wrestle in WWE. This effectively killed Copani's career, as he was forever associated with the Hassan character. He left the business shortly thereafter, and his life took a severe downturn, as he now works the worst possible job you could imagine: as a principal at a junior high school in Hannibal, New York. You can only imagine that some days, he would be much more at ease dealing with chair-swinging madmen and psychotic fans than unruly kids and privileged parents.

ECW *High Incident* 1996: Since its founding in 1992, Extreme Championship Wrestling (ECW) continuously pushed the envelope by featuring more outrageous moments than its competitors, with shows regularly including over-the-top violence, steel chairs, barbed wire, and a steady supply of established veterans and young, hungry talent trying their damnedest every night to make their mark in the industry. That, plus a newer hybrid of traditional mat wrestling and the breakneck daredevil stylings of Japanese strong style and Mexican lucha libre, led to a small though rabid fanbase. ECW had everything that fans who didn't like the older, more established wrestling federations could hope for. Its angles and feuds were also more risqué, with regular storylines involving infidelity, lesbianism, cultism, and more.

One such feud featured a character named Raven—the tough, sadistic leader of a grunge-themed group of violent outcasts. He got involved in a war with another wrestler named the Sandman, a beer-drinking, cigarette-smoking, Singapore cane-swinging psychopath who would attack anyone put in front of him. The feud escalated when Raven not only started dating the Sandman's ex-wife, but the Sandman's eight-year-old son started dressing and acting like Raven. Attacks on the Sandman by Raven's followers were common, as was his swinging that cane around and hitting the bejeezus out of everyone.

ECW's main show that month was called ECW *High Incident* '96. It featured a full card of excellent talent and great matches, and if not for one small incident, the show could have been considered one of the best that ECW held that year. What was that one small incident? The Sandman was defending the ECW Heavyweight title against another wrestler, 2 Cold Scorpio, when Raven and his followers attacked him. Using a bracing board (a reinforcing board) as a makeshift cross, they then "crucified" the Sandman by tying him to the board with barbed wire and even making a crown of thorns out of the barbed wire for the Sandman to wear, all while the Sandman's wife laughed and his son watched. The usually unruly crowd, which regularly cheered for the bad guys, was strangely silent—a huge clue that something was wrong. A short time later, Raven came back out to the ring and uncharacteristically apologized for the angle, something he had never done before.

Speaking of angle, Olympic Gold medalist and future WWE superstar Kurt Angle made his first appearance in the wrestling ring that night. At the time, Angle had been considering wrestling for ECW; however, what had taken place that night made him so furious that he told ECW President Paul Heyman he was leaving. He also told Heyman that if any footage leaked with his image attached to the incident, Heyman would be hearing from Angle's lawyers. Needless to say, footage of that event was stricken from future viewing, although the individual matches were used on many best-of compilations. The crucifixion angle was so unpopular that no wrestling federation ever did it again...until the WWF did a variation of it with Steve Austin and the Undertaker in '98...and once more with Stephanie McMahon and the Undertaker that same month. Wow.

Katie Vick: Few moments have rallied wrestling fans against something as much as this one did. At the time, a feud between Triple H and Kane, the Undertaker's kayfabe brother—who was burned in a fire when he was younger—was WWE's main push, but it wasn't really selling with the audience. During a promo on *Monday Night Raw*, Triple H said he'd discovered that Kane had a crush on a girl named Katie Vick, but she was killed in a car accident. Triple H then tried to blackmail Kane into dropping the match, saying that he'd found footage of Kane having sex with her *after* she died. When the footage was shown, it was Triple H dressed like Kane and having fake sex with a mannequin in a coffin, even scooping slime out of the dummy's head and saying, "I (BEEP)ed her brains out!" The angle was immediately despised. In fact, it was so hated that it was dropped two weeks after they did it. Yessir, no angles could bring in the money like necrophilia.

Monsters: Real-world issues have killed careers immediately, while some crimes have gone unnoticed for decades before coming to light. The following are some names that Peacock will likely avoid altogether due to events outside the ring.

Buck "Rock 'n' Roll" Zumhofe: Trained by legendary American Wrestling Association (AWA) owner Verne Gagne in a class that included both the Iron Sheik and Ricky Steamboat, Zumhofe wrestled from 1972 to 2014. In '86, he was jailed for three years for sexual misconduct involving a minor. In 2013, he was sent to prison again, this time for 25 years, for sexually abusing his daughter.

Chris "the Crippler" Benoit: On June 24, 2007, WWE superstar Chris Benoit killed himself after killing his wife, Nancy, and his seven-year-old son, Daniel. This horrific double murder/suicide sent shockwaves through the wrestling industry, as it opened multiple media-led investigations into how drug abuse, crime, harassment, and the like are treated behind the scenes of pro-wrestling. The Sports Legacy Institute suggested that, besides experiencing severe depression caused by no less than eight of his close friends dying within a 19-month period, Benoit suffered from chronic traumatic encephalopathy, a result of brain damage caused by the multiple concussions he had suffered over his 20-plus years in the business. After examining Benoit's brain, the Institute said that the damage was equal to "an 85-year-old with dementia." WWE did not accept that conclusion in the least and has since removed Benoit from most of its history, with the exception of multi-star events from which he could not be cut. Peacock will likely just cut those segments altogether.

Hardbody Harrison/Harrison Norris, Jr.: Operation Desert Shield and Operation Desert Storm veteran Harrison Norris, Jr., debuted as a preliminary wrestler for WCW in '95, even wrestling at WCW's premiere pay-per-view event, *Starrcade*, in 1997. After WWE purchased WCW in 2001, Norris retired from pro-wrestling. In 2007, he was arrested for keeping eight women as sex slaves. He was subsequently convicted of forced labor, human trafficking, witness tampering, criminal conspiracy, and obstruction of justice, among other charges. He is currently serving life in prison.

Terry Garvin: Terry Garvin was a longtime industry veteran who, in the '80s, worked his way up the ranks of WWF management. His career ended when a scandal broke about his sexually harassing young rookies and blackmailing them into sex. Because he was a closeted homosexual, Pat Patterson was dragged into the scandal, but those charges were false, while the ones levied against Garvin were not. Garvin was fired, and his name has never been brought up since.

Invader No. 1/José González: Longtime Puerto Rican mainstay José González debuted for the World Wrestling Council (WWC) and found success as both a talent and a booker. In '88, González took issue with professional wrestler Bruiser Brody, which led to him stabbing Brody to death in a locker room. He was charged with murder; however, key witnesses disappeared after being threatened, other witnesses received court summons *after* the trial had concluded, and the murder weapon mysteriously disappeared, which was convenient considering the WWC management's ties to the local police department. After González was found not guilty of the blatant murder, the WWC used that same murder as a storyline for González's character. Later, González tried but failed to enter politics. He retired in 2014 and, one year later, was inducted into the Salón de los Inmortales, the World Wrestling League's hall of fame.

Bruiser Bedlam/Ion Croitoru: Ion Croitoru (aka Taras Bulba, aka Johnny K-9 in WWF rings in the '80s) was a well-known preliminary wrestler who never found great success. After Croitoru joined Smoky Mountain Wrestling in '92, owner/promoter/booker Jim Cornette did what he did with a lot of underutilized talent and reinvented Croitoru's character as Bruiser Bedlam, a hard-nosed bodyguard for the tag team the Heavenly Bodies (Tom Prichard and Jimmy Del Rey). At one point, he scored a pinfall victory over visiting WWF talent Randy "Macho Man" Savage. When Smoky Mountain Wrestling folded in late '95, Bruiser Bedlam drifted between federations, usually working smaller indie shows. He soon joined the Satan's Choice biker gang and was later convicted of cocaine trafficking, extortion, assault, and the bombing of a police station (The last offense was revenge for getting kicked out of a strip club). He was eventually charged with the execution-style murders of two people but was found not guilty, although he did plead guilty to a plethora of other charges. After joining the United Nations gang, he was arrested for conspiracy to commit the murder of several members of the Red Scorpions gang. In 2011, he was charged with attempted murder and kidnapping. He made parole in 2015. After his release, Croitoru got married, worked as a bodyguard for Lion's Gate Entertainment, and even landed a few acting jobs. In 2017, he died in a federal halfway house at the age of 53.

Steve "Gatorwolf"/Stephen Ketcher: Stephen Ketcher was a WWWF veteran pushed as an "Indian" wrestler akin to Chief Jay Strongbow, although, like Strongbow, Ketcher wasn't a bit Native American. At the height of his push, he forgot to do the traditional "Indian War Dance" in celebration of his victory, which dropped him down to preliminary wrestler status. However, cutting him down in stature turned out to be a blessing in disguise, as he would later be jailed for repeatedly sexually assaulting a 15-year-old friend of his daughter.

"Nightmare" Ken Wayne: In the '80s, Ken Wayne formed a semi-successful tag team with Danny Davis called the Nightmares. He was a moderately successful journeyman wrestler and trainer for the WWF, which earned him some prelim matches with the WWF and WCW. In 2015, a police raid on his home turned up massive amounts of child pornography. This earned him a 20-year sentence, five of which he served in prison, while the remaining 15 were served under post-release supervision.

STEREOTYPES

Because costumes can often tell a story much quicker than a verbal or written explanation, stereotypes have long been the bread and butter of professional wrestling. Sure, a 1980s wrestler standing in the middle of the ring in simple trunks and boots can get noticed through toughness and skill, but that won't make the audience care for him at all. Now, if that same wrestler wears red clothes, dons red boots, and waves a Soviet flag while yelling some Russian words he heard on TV once? That guy is instantly hated and, as such, has the power to draw people who want to see his ass kicked. The following identifies some of the more infamous stereotypes used in wrestling over the years and discusses how they look through today's eyes.

Nazi Wrestlers: One of the first notable villains/heels of televised wrestling appeared in the '50s. Hans Schmidt was an "evil German" who always battled the heroes in the ring. Born Guy Larose in Québec, Canada, he became infamous for terrorizing the wrestling rings as a rough, cheating bad guy, although he never actually wore Nazi symbols. Karl Von Hess, whose real name was Frank Fakety, was a World War II veteran from Omaha, Nebraska, who took Schmidt's gimmick a step further. He came off as an actual Nazi sympathizer, wearing a cape printed with the Iron Cross, which made him a nationally hated figure. This led to big profits for the wrestling industry, as many waited in line with cash in hand to see someone kick his ass. James Raschke (aka Baron von Raschke), also a military veteran from Omaha, went full-bore Nazi with his gimmick, goose-stepping, throwing out the salute, and even wearing a cape with a swastika on it. When he appeared again as a heel in later years, he had dropped the Nazi gimmick for the same reason most of the others did: They were tired of getting stabbed at or attacked with weapons when they wrestled…or shopped with their kids…or ate at a diner. Back then, most of the world thought wrestling was real, so if you were a veteran and this Nazi came into a store you were in, and you had just happened to have lost friends to people like this…. You can see situations escalating quickly. The most famous of these angles

Boo the Evil Baron Von Raschke! (All photos this section stolen. Photographers unknown. All Rights Reserved.)

involved the legendary Von Erich family, consisting of brothers Fritz and Waldo. Fritz (real name Jack Adkisson, from Texas) and Waldo (real name Walter Sieber, from Toronto, Canada) infuriated fans in the ring from the late '50s on as Nazi sympathizers who would randomly throw out the salute to get more heat. In the '70s, Waldo semi-retired to a partial work schedule. Fritz then recanted his Nazi-sympathizing ways, explaining that he had been "thinking wrong" over the years. By this time, the Nazi gimmick had almost completely disappeared from the wrestling business, replaced by more villains coming from areas like the Eastern Bloc, Asia, the Middle East, Australia—any place that was unfamiliar to North American fans. Villainous Englishmen popped up every now and again, but unlike some of the aforementioned wrestlers, most of them were really English.

RACIAL

Playing up to a stereotype is, at best, a risky proposition despite any good intentions. Some members of the casts of Mel Brooks's *Blazing Saddles* and Quentin Tarantino's *Django Unchained* wandered across some dicey situations and dialogue that they said made them uncomfortable. The following provides some glaring examples of successful gimmicks that not only tread the precarious line of decency, but crossed it, stomped on it, and set it on fire.

Nicknamed "the Ugandan Giant," Kamala, who was born in Mississippi and whose real name was James Harris, was an African-American wrestler who started his career as "Sugar Bear" Harris in the late '70s. However, he didn't achieve much success as a journeyman. Upon returning to the United States after a tour overseas, he became involved with the Continental Wrestling Association. There, he, Jerry "the King" Lawler, and promoter Jerry Jarrett drew upon different ideas, finally coming up with the Kamala gimmick: a vicious Ugandan headhunter who's adapted his savagery to the "outside" world and who once served as a bodyguard for exiled Ugandan President Idi Amin. The subsequent promotional video showed Kamala painted up to mimic imagery from a Frank Frazetta painting; he also wore a loincloth, held a spear, and looked bloodthirsty as hell as he emerged from a steamy African jungle while his manager, J.J. Dillon, said that no one was safe from Kamala. Of course, none of the audience knew that the

*Kamala the Headhunter and "Friend." So...not offensive at all.
(Again, these photos arrived by unknown courier late at night. All Rights Reserved.)*

African jungle shown in the video was Hendersonville, Tennessee, and the fog coming out of the "steamy" jungle was dry ice. The locale was just as fabricated as the character, but audience members believed they were seeing an actual monster. He wrestled like a monster too, delivering clubbing punches and biting his opponents bloody. Just in case that didn't perpetuate the stereotype enough, he never spoke English while in character. He also attacked anyone near him (usually referees and officials), came to the ring with "tribal" music playing in the background, and was always escorted by his own personal handlers, who would often wave their arms to distract him or occasionally cover his head with a hood to calm him down. This gimmick lasted from 1982 until Kamala's retirement in 1996.

The tag team the Wild Samoans was composed of two Samoan "wild men" brothers, Afa and Sika. What sets them apart from most is that they were *actually* from Western Samoa, *actually* brothers, and *actually* named Afa Anoa'i, Sr., and Sika Anoa'i (respectively). They always kept a monstrous demeanor, sporting wild, unkept afros and never wearing shoes. They also attacked their opponents with brutal abandon and never spoke English unless alone or in the company of family or coworkers. A famous story involves them getting arrested by the police over a situation that could have been easily explained, but in doing so, they would have given away their real characters and identities. Though they portrayed these nightmarish figures on television, they were shrewd businessmen behind the scenes. They founded the Wild Samoans Training Center, which trained some of the biggest names in wrestling, including Bam Bam Bigelow, Batista, Sherri Martel, Michael Hayes, and Yokozuna—quite surprising for a duo who tore apart and ate raw fish in interviews.

Another notable name is Saba Simba, a character that Tony White, originally from Virginia, brought to the ring in 1990. Simba wrestled in full African Zulu regalia and did a traditional Zulu dance. The character was acknowledged on television as originally being Tony Atlas, who had "rediscovered his roots" and changed his name and look accordingly. Audiences didn't look upon the character too fondly, and Simba never rode higher than mid-card status throughout his run, with one critic even writing that the gimmick was "unpopular at best and racist at worst." As awkward as the gimmick was, White credited the Simba role with saving his life, stating that he was homeless at the time when he was called back to the WWF.

In 1986, a newly arrived WWF talent named Slick (real name Ken Johnson) was a streetwise manager who dressed in flashy suits, drove expensive cars, and spoke in exaggerated jive. His most eye-raising moment involved a music video he made for "Jive Soul Bro," the song he did for the WWF's *Piledriver: The Wrestling Album II*. In the extended video, Slick is shown eating fried chicken and asking to "eat his yard bird in peace" before introducing the song. The video shows him strutting, cane in hand, down a predominantly

African-American neighborhood and being equally praised and ridiculed by its occupants. The most damning thing about the song is that it's catchy as hell, and I dare you not to hum it if you know it. (On a side note: The song was actually a cover of another song called "Jive Ol' Fo," by hip-hop artist Captain Chameleon.) Slick managed heels in the WWF until he left in 1993. Having retired from his career with the WWF, he earned bachelor's and master's degrees from Campbellsville University and is now an ordained minister in Kentucky.

Professional wrestler Charles Wright was gifted with a large build and impressive height, which, when added to an array of tattoos, gave him an intimidating appearance. Wright's ability to adapt quickly to the wrestling business was a definite plus, and he excelled enough to get noticed by the WWF in late '91, just two years after he began wrestling. After a few years in the WWF and a couple unsuccessful but memorable personas (for example, voodoo priest Papa Shango), Wright was repackaged again, this time without any gimmicks, under the name Kama Mustafa. He joined a Black militant-themed group called the Nation of Domination as a respected member. During interviews, he picked up the nickname "the Godfather" and kept it when the group disbanded. After that, he went by the Godfather professionally and debuted a pimp-style change of wardrobe, complete with gold chains, a derby hat, gold-framed glasses, and a "pimp cane." He also premiered a running entourage of scantily clad ladies (made up of up-and-coming female wrestlers and actual exotic dancers) he called his "hos," who would accompany and dance with him on the way to the ring. Oh, and the pimp imagery didn't just end there; he would get on the mic and tell the ladies to "get on the hooooooooo train" (said the same way as the opening of *Soul Train*). Heavily influenced by late '70s funk, his theme music echoed the "ho train" line and was the feather in the pimp hat of the overall image. The Godfather remained incredibly popular throughout his initial run, though he once turned heel by renouncing his sinful ways and joining a wrestling stable called Right to Censor, a group made up of kayfabe right-wing conservative wrestlers. The fans absolutely hated this angle, and when he returned with the "hos" as the Godfather, the cheers where deafening. He lightened his career after that, leaving WWE and working sporadically at house shows, always with the Godfather gimmick, although he did have to change his name to Pimp Fatha for legal issues. He still makes appearances with WWE, although he has almost given up wrestling entirely, reserving the gimmick for wrestling reunions,

Akeem the Dream and his manager, Slick.

conventions, and, er, judging exotic dance contests at strip clubs.

And then there's the tag team the Gangstas, made up of wrestlers New Jack (Jerome Young) and Mustafa Saed (Jamal Mustafa), who premiered in Jim Cornette's southern-based Smoky Mountain Wrestling in '94. The duo dressed like L.A. gang members and cut promos on O.J. Simpson and Louis Farrakhan to infuriate the crowd. They would eat watermelon and fried chicken, with a 40-ounce bottle of malt liquor just in camera shot. At the same time, they would laugh at how "stupid crackers think this is what we do" and how they only had to win matches via pinfall with a two-count rather than a three "because affirmative action says we can." Amazingly enough, their actions and interviews only escalated when they went to Paul Heyman's Philadelphia-based ECW, where their angry, expletive-heavy interviews only endeared them to that crowd. (Philly is an…unusual place, and let's leave it at that.) Adding to their image was that they played Dr. Dre and Ice Cube's "Natural Born Killers" continuously during their matches, making each one appear almost like a music video.

In case one thinks those kinds of stereotypes are things of the past in wrestling, there are more recent examples to reference. An over-the-top parody of a gangster duo, Cryme Tyme was composed of JTG/Jayson Anthony Paul and Shad Gaspard, who wrestled together from 2010 to 2014. There's also the Mexicools, a three-man tag team of famous Mexican wrestlers Psicosis, Super Crazy, and Juventud Guerrera. With Latin music playing in the background, this trio drove out to the ring atop a riding lawnmower they called a "Juan Deere" (although they were just following the example set by fellow Mexican wrestler Konnan years prior, who swapped his flamboyant, lucha-inspired tights for baggy Dickies, wifebeaters, bandanas, and sunglasses to accentuate his "gang look").

CULTURAL APPROPRIATION

Cultural appropriation is when one culture inappropriately adopts something that is indicative of another culture's identity. It's especially problematic when a more prevalent culture inappropriately takes from a minority culture. It's been practiced in Hollywood over the years in ways that range from **meant no offense whatsoever** (Hank Azaria as Apu on *The Simpsons*) to **what the hell were they thinking** (Mickey Rooney as Mr. Yunioshi in *Breakfast at Tiffany's*)? The world of pro-wrestling is no different.

Italian American Luke Scarpa wrestled on the East Coast and in the South for years, winning some championships along the way but never becoming a major draw. That changed in 1970 when he began working in the WWF as Chief Jay Strongbow, billed as a Native American wrestler. Strongbow wore a feathered ceremonial headdress in addition to his traditional wrestling attire. He also did a "tribal war dance" and used a series of "Indian chops" to attack his opponents. In the '70s, one of Strongbow's regular tag team partners was "fellow Native American" wrestler Billy White Wolf. The problem here was that Billy's real name was

Adnan Al-Kaissie, and he was Iraqi, not Native American. He was even childhood friends with Saddam Hussein. He dropped the Native American gimmick when it turned out the money he made as a hero/baby face paled in comparison to the money he made as "Sheik" Adnan Al-Kaissie, known then as a Middle Eastern madman bent on destroying Americans.

Ivan Koloff, the "Russian Bear"—perhaps the most famous of the Soviet heels in pro-wrestling—was born Oreal Perras in Québec and was French Canadian as hell. In 1984, Koloff was tasked with training a young, incredibly muscled, but very green rookie sent "by the Soviets to bolster Koloff's mission of sports dominance." This man was Scott Simpson, but the wrestling world knew him as the "Russian Nightmare," Nikita Koloff. The two, along with American turncoat Krusher Kruschev (real name Barry Darsow), formed a three-man unit that drew both huge heat and big box office receipts from audiences nationwide. These "Russians" were so hated that promoters learned that placing them even against other villains was profitable, just so long as someone—anyone—could stop this Soviet menace. Other famous "Russians" in wrestling include:

- Boris Zhukov (real name James Harrell, from Roanoke, Virginia)
- Soldat Ustinov (real name Jim Lanning, from Minneapolis, Minnesota)
- Vladimir Petrov (real name Al Blake, also from Minneapolis, Minnesota)
- Russian Assassin #1 (real name David Sheldon, from Arlington, Texas)
- Russian Assassin #2 (real name Ken Rinehurst [aka Jack Victory], from Atlantic City, New Jersey)
- Nikolai Volkoff, whose real name was Josip Peruzović and who was from Croatia, which is not Russia, mind you, but is the closest you'll get with this list (Volkoff actually spoke with a heavy Croatian accent in real life, but the other "Russians" here usually spoke with a suspiciously Midwestern drawl.)

One WWF tag team to emerge in the early '90s was called the Orient Express and featured Akio Sato (from Hokkaido, Japan) and Pat Tanaka (from Honolulu, Hawaii). They wore red robes to the ring and were always accompanied by their manager, Mr. Fuji. In his managerial role, Mr. Fuji, a Japanese heel from the '60s and '70s, was sneaky and underhanded as anything, but he did cut a memorable image with his tuxedo, bow tie, bowler hat, and cane. Tanaka had just signed with the WWF, leaving his longtime partner, Paul Diamond, behind in the American Wrestling Association. Tanaka and Diamond, a 6-foot-2 Croatian whose real name is Thomas Boric, had wrestled as a very successful tag team called Badd Company. Diamond was signed to the WWF later that same year, but he worked mostly as enhancement talent, highlighting the abilities of other wrestlers.

When Sato abruptly decided to retire from in-ring work, it seemed that all the WWF had to do was reunite Tanaka and Diamond as Badd Company. The WWF did reunite the two, but it kept them under the name the Orient Express, with Diamond now being called Kato and wearing a mask to hide the fact that he wasn't Japanese. In interviews, Diamond usually only nodded, bowed, or said, "Hai!" What's worse is that Badd Company had a huge catalogue of moves and double-team maneuvers its members had learned over the years, but as the Orient Express, they had to use more "traditional" Japanese actions (karate chops, kicks, and so on). Even limited by these actions, Tanaka and Diamond were known as real work horses for a couple of years, putting over up-and-coming talent and making the audience happy (or in this case, unhappy). The team officially broke up when Tanaka left in '92.

One of the last examples of cultural appropriation appeared in the '90s with the WWF's most feared competitor: Yokozuna, a 500-plus-pound Japanese sumo wrestler who threw people around like rag dolls. His real name was Agatupu Anoa'i, of the famous Samoan Anoa'i family, and he wrestled under his Samoan name for years before joining the WWF. The WWF and Vince McMahon wanted a new "foreign threat," and the Russian and Middle Eastern angles had recently been done. Several Japanese heels had come before, but at this time, Japan was in the news for aggressive business tactics. These real-world squabbles were fertile soil for the WWF to make a perfect heel for the '90s, and so Yokozuna was born: a six-foot-four giant who wore sumo robes and regalia, while his manager, Mr. Fuji, carried a ceremonial salt bucket and waved a Japanese flag before matches. By this time, Mr. Fuji had abandoned the tuxedo getup for a shaved head and flowing Japanese robes; getting paired with Yokozuna only added to the overall image. The gimmick was a huge success, with Yokozuna winning the WWF Championship and placing at the top of cards and pay-per-views for a time. Eventually, he was used as supplemental talent to put over rising stars.

George Gray was a six-foot-nine man who weighed in around the 400-pound mark. In late '82, he adopted the image of a monstrous biker, complete with a mohawk, tattoos on the side of his bare scalp, leather gloves, denim vests, and the name the One-Man Gang. This persona proved to be an intimidating heel and a solid moneymaking journeyman in several territories. He signed with the WWF as the same character in '87 and had several successful runs against some of the top baby faces in the company.

However, in late '88, the WWF creative thought the One-Man Gang character needed something new. The solution was to use an angle where Gang's manager, Slick, found out that Gang's family had roots in Africa and sought to have the wrestler embrace his heritage. WWF interviewer Gene Okerlund was invited to witness this revelation and took a camera crew on location: an unnamed ghetto alleyway. In that alleyway, which Slick called the "deepest, darkest parts of Africa," Slick, Okerlund, and the crew stood around a burning trashcan, while performers dressed in African tribal clothing danced in the background. A huge puff of smoke came from the can, and Slick yelled, "Behold! Akeem, the African Dream!"

The One-Man Gang appeared, his normal biker clothes discarded for a large dashiki and a kufi cap. Akeem immediately started talking in exaggerated jive and walking with a pronounced strut, and he sometimes danced just to himself. It sounds much more insulting than it probably is, but honestly, it was just so stupid that people couldn't get past rolling their eyes to be offended.

HOMOSEXUAL ANGLES

It goes without saying that a majority of the typical wrestling audience teemed (and still teems) with what is now considered toxic masculinity. The male performers were always supposed to be strong and aggressive, and the women were mostly beautiful and not involved in the action, with the exception of valets, managers, and the rare female wrestler. If a male wrestler acted weak or feminine in any way, he was labeled a "sissy" and subsequently embarrassed. Male managers were typically treated this way, acting sneaky and getting their just desserts for interfering in the heroes' matches, but any wrestlers who acted weak or feminine got instant heat from the crowd.

"The Exotic One," a Welshman named Adrian Street, was a double-tough wrestler who became famous in the '80s for his androgynous persona, bright makeup, flamboyant outfits, and bleached-blond hair, which he kept up in pigtails. He had a similarly adorned valet named Miss Linda, who would interfere when needed but was primarily there to treat his robes and fix his hair. Wrestling had had "pretty boys" prior to Street, but Street's use of double entendres and habit of holding onto wrestlers "a little too long" to unnerve them was something that had never been seen before. Similarly, the WWF also had an established veteran named Adrian Adonis, who replaced his black clothes for pastels and became a cross-dresser (with hints of being a homosexual) in the ring.

Dustin Runnels left WCW in '96 and reinvented himself in the WWF as Goldust, an androgynous wrestler covered from head to toe in gold. He flirted with opponents and pinned them in suggestive or odd ways. The character was a hit, with half the crowd hating him and half eager to see what he would do next. Similarly, in WCW in '99, two preliminary wrestlers named Lenny and Lodi fully embraced the gay image, calling themselves the West Hollywood Blondes. They suddenly became popular and were about to receive a push when Turner Network ordered WCW to shut the angle down immediately. Likewise, Chuck Palumbo and Billy Gunn, otherwise known as Billy and Chuck (accompanied by their flamboyant manager, Rico), pushed the "Are they?/Aren't they?" angle pretty hard. This led to a marriage proposal and, later, an officiated wedding ceremony on *SmackDown*. Just before they tied the knot, the two men disavowed being gay, saying that the entire thing was a publicity stunt. Of course, they were immediately attacked by a tag team known as Three-Minute Warning, and the old preacher who was to marry them turned out to be former WCW President Eric Bischoff in a *Scooby-Doo*-worthy unmasking… but that goes without saying.

OTHER POSSIBLY OFFENSIVE STEREOTYPES

Though the following received little criticism at the time, through modern eyes, they could be viewed as problematic. For instance, there were heritage/nationality-related stereotypes. Japanese wrestlers in U.S. rings always spoke using broken English. They also dressed in ceremonial robes and almost always delivered karate chops and kicks, even if the wrestler in question had no formal marital arts training. The first wrestler to fully embrace the aesthetic of both martial arts cinema and Japanese theatre was the Great Kabuki (Akihisa Mera, from Miyazaki, Japan). Throughout the '70s, he would appear wearing black karategi trousers, his fingers and feet taped, his hair long and sometimes top-knotted, and his face painted in a demon Kabuki-style pattern. The overall look was sometimes accentuated by an Omatsuri- or Hannya-style demon mask and overextending wig. The fact that he never spoke added to the mystery surrounding his character. His weapons were also symbolically Asian, and he was proficient with wrapped shinai, bamboo canes, and nunchakus. However, what made him famous in the industry was that he was the first wrestler to use "Asian mist," a mysterious spray he could spit into his opponents' eyes at almost any time. Blinded, his competitors would collapse with their hands over eyes, screaming for someone to help them. The announcers rightfully vilified this horrible cheating, noting that they didn't know what was in the mist. Perhaps it was made of "mysterious heated spices from the Orient" that would set your tastebuds aflame, so who knows what it would do to your eyes? When asked about the Asian mist, Kabuki's manager, Gary Hart, merely said, "It is a secret, known for thousands of years, stemming from feudal Japan, and those in the United States will never know it." Well, here, now, for those reading, is the secret of the Asian mist: It's Kool-Aid...or candy...or colored mints—anything Kabuki could hide until needing to use it. Sometimes, he'd even keep a bottle of whatever under the ring; during a fight, he would take an unnoticed sip and was ready to go.

In late '89, Japanese wrestler Keiji Mutoh signed with WCW under the name the Great Muta. He adopted a lot of Kabuki's traits, even signing the same manager, Gary Hart, which worked out well since he never spoke during interviews either. He also wore the same style of ring gear, painted his face, and did the mist gimmick, but his overall look emulated ninjutsu wardrobe more than Kabuki-style garments, and he was much more athletic and agile than the Great Kabuki. Regardless, he was introduced as the Great Kabuki's son, even though the two were not related.

The Moondogs also emerged in the '80s. The tag team was made up of journeymen wrestlers who could adopt the name as long as they looked the part, which included wearing blue-jean cut-off shorts; having wild, unkempt hair and beards; wearing no shoes; and always chewing on bones in interviews or on their way to the ring. They were named after dogs (Rex, Spot, etc.) and usually growled or howled at announcers rather

Kerwin White. On his off-days when not beating folks to death with his bare hands.

than speak. The crowd considered them backwoods rednecks and/or "poor white trash," with some in the audience even singing the banjo theme from the movie *Deliverance* when they appeared. Many, **many** Moondogs have popped up in the indie circuit over the years, but the first one ever was Lonnie Mayne, aka Moondog Mayne, who started the gimmick in '73. He died in '78, and in '80, Randy Colley picked up the mantle and character type as Moondog Rex, joining Moondog King (Ed White) in the WWF. Over the years, there have been 24 (!) Moondogs in addition to the original five, including a few female ones and an African-American Moondog named—wait for it—Big Black Dog. Yeesh.

Salvador Guerrero IV, known to the wrestling world as Chavo Guerrero, Jr., was a well-respected professional wrestler from the legendary Guerrero family, and while never reaching main-event status, he was involved in many great angles and matches due to management and the audience's appreciation for his work rate and abilities. The audience found Chavo to be a perfect complement and tag partner to his real-life superstar uncle, Eddie Guerrero. Because members of the Guerrero family were always outspokenly proud of their Hispanic heritage, it was a shock when, after he and Eddie disbanded as a tag team, Chavo showed up with blonde hair and no Hispanic accent, dressing and acting, well, white, and even changing his name to Kerwin White. Golf clubs in hand, he drove to the ring in a golf cart and made off-hand remarks about Hispanics, African Americans, Asian Americans, Native Americans, and just basically anyone who wasn't Caucasian. Neither the fans nor Chavo liked the bit, but like always, in wrestling, you did what you were told. The angle disappeared a few months later, not due to rational thinking from the creative, but because Eddie died for real. Chavo dropped the gimmick immediately and returned to being just Chavo.

OFFENSIVE ANGLES

Some storylines trod up to the line of decency and pulled back right before they got distasteful. Others not only crossed the line, but set it on fire and urinated on it to put it out. Some of the more awful ones are listed below.

Originally from St. Joseph, Missouri, Ed Wiskoski wrestled under his given name from '73 to '85, making decent money as a journeyman and winning a title here and there. By the time he went to the AWA in '85, the organization had begun to nosedive due to many of its big-name talent going to either the WWF or the NWA. As a result, the AWA needed a ready-made heel who could be hated immediately. The result was a character named Colonel DeBeers, a pro-apartheid, military-styled madman hailing from Cape Town, South Africa. Keep in mind that South African apartheid issue had just been thrust into the limelight front and center after a group of singers made a protest song similar to what the U.S. had done for Africa with "We are the World." This song was called "Sun City," and it went into heavy rotation on MTV. (Do you want to know the singers involved? Well, too bad, because they're too many to list here.) In interviews, DeBeers was blatant about his hatred of "lesser races"; even in a business that used racism as a tool, something this vile was shocking to see. He would refuse matches against African-American wrestlers and even grew furious at white wrestlers who would tag team with them. He also got into a feud with popular superstar Jimmy "Superfly" Snuka, pushing him off the top rope to the floor below the ring and repeatedly bashing his head against the concrete. This led to an extended feud that sold some tickets, though nowhere near as many as the AWA had expected. DeBeers ran as a hated figure until he retired the character in the early 2000s.

Examples of Extreme Violence: Violence has always been a part of professional wrestling, but on occasion, the action has gone too far. Here is a list of some of the bloodier incidents:

- Road Warriors using a spike on Dusty Rhodes's eye
- Fantastics vs. Sheepherder (barbed wire matches)
- Kevin Sullivan vs. WING Kanemura (attack)
- Tommy Rich vs. Buzz Sawyer (feud)
- Dusty Rhodes vs. Ric Flair or Dusty Rhodes vs. Tully Blanchard
- Terry Funk vs. Sabu (barbed wire match)
- Bruiser Brody vs. Abdullah the Butcher (any match of theirs, really)

Bill Watts's Mid-South Wrestling was based heavily in the lower South and Midwest regions, particularly Oklahoma, Louisiana, Mississippi, and Arkansas. At the time, the business was still segregated in terms of wrestling talent. Behind the scenes, management acting as promoters did very little to extend opportunities to non-whites. Watts realized that the territory to which he catered had a large African-American audience, so he booked accordingly. He regularly included Black athletes in major angles. He even included them in main-event matches, enabling them to fight for the NWA World title whenever a reigning world champion came through. Other promoters were furious at this, but Watts didn't care, as "the only color that matters is green."

There have been conflicting reports over the years regarding Watts's own prejudice; regardless, he regularly hired African Americans for management, most notably hiring "Big Cat" Ernie Ladd as a booker, which, besides accountant, is the most trusted job you could have for a promoter. That said, there is no mistaking that some of the promos and angles in Mid-South went too far, even for back then. For instance, journeymen wrestlers "Dirty" Dutch Mantel and Tom Pritchard had a quasi-Western look accentuated by the bullwhip that Dutch carried with him. If they had more trouble than usual with someone, they sprawled the defeated opponent out and whipped them. They did this on numerous occasions to Caucasian wrestlers, but one night, Black wrestler Mike Reagan embarrassed them during a tag team match. As they prepared to whip him, another African-American wrestler nicknamed the Snowman hit the ring and chased them off, taking the whip from them. The subsequent promo cut, while admittedly poorly done, made no mistake in letting the audience know what it was supposed to be feeling, with the Snowman stating, "It ain't 1824 anymore!"

Degeneration X: Degeneration X, or just DX, was a group made up of white wrestlers Triple H, X-Pac, "Road Dogg" Jesse James, "Mr. Ass" Billy Gunn, and Chyna. They went around acting like punks/spoiled brats when they got into a feud with another group of mostly Black wrestlers called the Nation of Domination, which included Faarooq, the Godfather, D'Lo Brown, Owen Hart, and the Rock. One week in '98, DX, known for pushing the envelope, made fun of the NOD by impersonating them in front of a live audience. In case the verbal impersonations weren't enough, X-Pac donned blackface.

Oklahoma: In 1999, WWF writer/producers Ed Ferrara and Vince Russo left for WCW. Their ideas to make WCW's product better were a mixed bag and ultimately, a failure. In a desperate move to establish Ed as a heel, he came out as Oklahoma, a character dressed exactly like respected WWF announcer Jim Ross (Oklahoma is where Jim Ross resides). His impersonation of Ross included exaggerated mimicry of Ross's Bell's palsy, complete with slurred speech and drooping eye and lip. This angered not only the crowd, but many in the locker room who respected Ross.

Eugene: Early in his career, Nick Dinsmore wrestled for Ohio Valley Wrestling, which was then run by Jim Cornette and Danny Davis, two men with a track record of creating talent. Dinsmore was a bit of a savant in the wrestling business, as his timing and skills were leagues better than his years would lend. He was a natural in the business, knowing where the camera was at all times, taking care of other wrestlers in the ring, and making himself and his coworkers look good. He was moved up to WWE in 2004,

Eugene.

but instead of just letting him be Nick Dinsmore or some other character, the WWE creative came up with the idea of Eugene, a *special needs* character reminiscent of Cameron Diaz's brother in *There's Something about Mary*. Eugene would smile broadly, look around when people talked to him, pat his ear, stammer, and speak with some difficulty. Make no mistake about it: Although the wrestling industry had previously invented characters who were slow or animalistic (e.g., Dave Sullivan and Abdullah the Butcher), this time, they flat out insinuated that a character had an intellectual disability, and they played it for laughs. The character was surprisingly popular with the fans, and when Dinsmore was released from WWE in '07, he still portrayed a variation of the character (U-Gene) at indie house shows.

The Artist Formerly Known as Goldust: In '97, Dustin Runnels, Goldust's revealed identity, knew something was wrong when fans began to accept the sexually ambiguous wrestler. He stated that he hated the fans, and if they wanted Goldust, they were going to get something else. He started dressing and acting increasingly weird. He changed his in-ring name and appearance every week in accordance with someone in the news or someone he was wrestling, taking on that person's mannerisms and likeness. When he faced off against African-American wrestler 2 Cold Scorpio, he came out dressed in a fur coat, gold chains, an afro wig, and full blackface. The announcers tried to put this over as him just trying to be shocking, but the audience didn't care. He continued wrestling in WWE/the WWF until leaving in '99, although he has returned several times since.

Tim White's Suicide Attempts: WWE reporter Josh Mathews interviewed referee Tim White inside White's bar in Cumberland, Rhode Island, for a 2005 pay-per-view. The interview showed White massively drunk, complaining how a big match he'd recently refereed had ruined his life. He then grabbed a shotgun, walked off-screen, and fired, hoping to kill himself. It was all an ill-advised skit, one made even worse by the fact that Eddie Guerrero had died just a few weeks before. It was later shown that he had (*ahem*) shot his foot and was fine. However, each week thereafter, WWE's website uploaded a new video every Thursday showing White trying and failing to kill himself when he'd cough out poison, a rope he was using to hang himself broke, and so on. The segment was even given a name: "Lunchtime Suicide." The segment went on for *14 weeks* (!) until they finally ended it with an upload showing White inviting Mathews back to his bar and accidentally shooting him.

PROMOS, COSTUMES, COMMENTARY, AND VERBAL MANEUVERS

In wrestling, cheap heat is getting an audience mad at you over simple insults, slurs, reactions, etc. To quickly establish themselves as heels back in the day, bad guys would drop slurs without batting an eye. The following are some characters of particular note.

Don Muraco: A feud with Pedro Morales led Don Muraco to crack anti-Mexican jokes on a daily basis. He did this even after someone pointed out to him that Morales was Puerto Rican.

Roddy Piper: In the '80s, "Rowdy" Roddy Piper played with racist taunts as fluently as Yo-Yo Ma plays the cello. The man was an artist at knowing the most awful thing to say at just the wrong time.

Jesse "the Body" Ventura: Previously a heel commentator for the WWF and WCW, Jesse Ventura used derogatory nicknames, particularly when discussing wrestlers Tito Santana and Koko B. Ware.

The Harley Race/Ron Simmons Confrontation: A seven-time former world champion, Harley Race took on the role of manager for WCW newcomer Big Van Vader in '91. At one point, Ron Simmons, an African-American wrestler finally getting a main-event push, was being interviewed in the ring by Jesse Ventura. Suddenly, Harley Race showed up with another wrestler named Super Invader (aka Hercules Hernandez) to berate Simmons. It was a typical wrestling interview right up until Race used the word "boy" and said they used to have guys like Simmons "carry our bags." Simmons instantly beat the hell out of both men, and it laid the groundwork for Simmons later winning the WCW World title from Vader, but it could have been done a thousand different ways better than this. WTBS had to have known the moment was coming, because it was beeped out the second it happened during the live telecast.

Bobby "the Brain" Heenan: Bobby Heenan was a commentator for the WWF and WCW, as well as being a longtime heel manager/advisor. He also used various nicknames, but he was funnier than hell and lightning-quick with verbal jabs, so, even when making some offensive jokes, he usually said them in such goofy ways that hating him was nearly impossible.

Jerry Lawler Promo on Goldust: Again, Goldust/Dustin Rhodes was a flamboyant, gold-costumed, (at best) sexually ambiguous character designed to shock and/or anger audiences with his mere presence. When Jerry "the King" Lawler cut a promo on Goldust, it contained Lawler's offensive use of a homophobic slur, as well as horrific insults targeting Goldust's wife and daughter.

The "Stars 'n' Bars": The Confederate flag has popped up over the years in many areas of entertainment, with the band Lynyrd Skynyrd and the television show *The Dukes of Hazzard* being perhaps the most prominent examples. Those who didn't know (or ignored) the history of the flag said they celebrated it as a symbol of "Southern pride." However, two things happened over the years:

1. The full history of the flag's symbolism became widespread public knowledge, so there's no mistaking what it stands for now.

2. White supremacists reclaimed the symbol with a passion.

Wrestlers who donned this flag in the ring include the Big Boss Man (Ray Traylor, Jr.), who wore a patch with the Georgia state flag on his arm; the tag team the Southern Boys (Tracy Smothers and Steve Armstrong); Dixie Dynamite, a masked wrestler *with the flag on his mask*; and most famously, the Fabulous Freebirds, a three-man, Southern-themed tag

The Fabulous Freebirds. All three proud members of the United States Senate.

team composed of Michael Hayes, Buddy Roberts, and Terry Gordy. The Fabulous Freebirds regularly wore shirts featuring the Confederate flag and even had matching, full-length robes with the Confederate flag decorating the entire back. Hayes said the reason they wore the symbol wasn't due to it being the Confederate flag, but because it was a very large part of the Georgia state flag and was "just gorgeous in color and design"—a design that, along with the Freebird logo, could easily be added to shirts, bandanas, and hats. Hayes has since disavowed the flag, as has everyone else mentioned here...well, except for Smothers, who wore it to the ring early in his career as a rebellious baby face and later wore it when working as a heel. "I'll wear it to get heat from crowds, especially Northern [crowds]. I'll wear my Full-Blooded Italian [another tag team he formed] shirts down South. [It] gets the same amount of heat down there!"

The Triple H/Booker T Promo: The promo leading into the Triple H/Booker T match at *WrestleMania XIX* was as unfortunate as they come, laden with racist subtext. Booker T, an immensely talented and universally respected African American and veteran wrestler, was getting a title shot against the champion Triple H at the next *WrestleMania* when Triple H began insulting Booker outright. He called Booker T's accomplishments in other federations a joke, talked about his opponent's "nappy" hair, and used phrasing like "somebody like...you" and "people like you." He later said that he was pointing out Booker T's (actual) criminal past, but he followed it up with some questionable actions and language in later weeks. The thing that really angered some viewers was that after all that buildup, it would have been some small justice if Booker T had won the match, but WWE didn't even let *that* happen, instead letting Triple H win at *WrestleMania*. This left many people upset and not in a way that translates to box office sales. Booker T won the belt a few years later, by the way.

JBL's Border Speech: In 2004, John "Bradshaw" Layfield, or simply JBL, was a 12-year veteran and longtime member of a hard-drinking, tough-as-nails, bone-breaking tag team called the APA (Acolytes Protection Agency). That year, Layfield's tag team partner, Faarooq (Ron Simmons), lightened his work schedule due to injuries sustained over the years, and Layfield decided to push his secondary career forward as a stock analyst. He developed a keen understanding of stock market response and, after making some wise investments, became wealthy. As a result, Layfield was regularly asked to share his views and evaluations of Wall Street on CNBC, Fox News, and Fox Business Network. He quickly changed from the long-haired, goateed wild man to a J.R. Ewing-esque entrepreneur, wearing Armani suits, eating fancy food, and calling the audience names for daring to be poor (since "only lazy people are poor"). A feud with then-WWE Champion Eddie Guerrero grew troublesome for the network when Layfield started disparaging Hispanic people for abiding undocumented immigrants. One promo featured Layfield looking for "illegal immigrants and freeloaders" at the actual border, a clip that also showed him harassing a kayfabe family trying to cross into the U.S. The people who shot the angle thought it successfully showcased JBL as an "asshole" and didn't expect the backlash that occurred when it was shown. Needless to say, the network contacted WWE immediately. However, the angle wasn't dropped, and JBL eventually won the belt from Guerrero, but the "border video" has rarely been discussed since.

THE FINAL BELL

All of these moments in professional wrestling will more than likely disappear when Peacock execs take one look at them. It's easy to see why some of these things are repulsive, and it's easy to blame the performers and/or management who thought them up. There are no excuses. However, if one had to pinpoint a common reason, in some cases, getting people to buy tickets for the next show was the difference between paying workers and shutting down operations altogether. The entire pro-wrestling industry is made up of throwing things at the wall and seeing what sticks. It's experimentation on an emotional, national, and financial scale; sometimes, it works, and sometimes, it doesn't. As for the performers, (in most cases) no one put a gun to their heads and made them do these things, so they have to be held accountable on some level. However, again, we must remember the times when these things occurred. In addition, many of these wrestlers never thought about the ramifications of playing these types of characters. They were just acting, no different from performers on Broadway or actors in films... nothing more, nothing less. Besides, if you didn't do it, someone else would happily step into your spot; you'd get punished for refusing, *and* that person would get your pay. Is that fair? Hell no. But what can you do?

That's just the business.

A Love Letter to Thunder Alley (1985) Interview with Jill Schoelen

By Dr. Rhonda Baughman

"I have always had a special love for this film," actress Jill Schoelen said of the 1985 film *Thunder Alley*. "As my career went on…you know, you kind of forget about the job you did before or the job you did three jobs earlier and four jobs earlier, but then, as time goes on…I would say that *Thunder Alley* is up there with a special love. It's a small film. It's a tiny, tiny film. At the time I was making it, I didn't have a lot to compare it to, but now…. I fully understood it was a small movie; however, there was an intimacy to the entire filmmaking process on a small film like that. I don't think that quality is necessarily unique to just *Thunder Alley* in my career, but I think it's just a normal feeling—that feeling of intimacy—on small films."

As Schoelen also said in our interview (and damn, does she say many great things): "The lifestyle choices we make following our dreams, how we stay small, and how we choose to grow big and let ourselves blossom—I think the drugs aspect of the film is a wonderful parallel story to people given the choices in their lives, because I think we always say we're afraid of failure, but sometimes, I think we're more afraid of success."

Rhonda: When you were shooting *Thunder Alley*, did you have any expectations for the film itself—that is, once it was released into the world, did you have thoughts, hopes, or desires attached to it?

Jill: Well, it was a really long time ago, but it was one of the very first movies that I ever did. I mean, the first movie I ever did was called *D.C. Cab*, for Universal. I was the love interest

I couldn't find some decent stills from Thunder Alley, so here's a shot of Jill from Popcorn. - ed.
© Studio Three Film. All Rights Reserved.

for the lead in that film, but it was a smaller, supporting role. I remember that getting *Thunder Alley* was exciting for me because it was a lead role and I was still so new to the business, to making movies and television. You know, it's funny: As an actor, you just go out and audition for jobs when you're young and trying to break into the business, and you're happy, whether it's television or film, for the most part. I was just very lucky, very fortunate to be able to make movies in the '80s, because the movies were what was important. Television really wasn't the way it is now. I mean, it was great to get a big network TV show, but there were only a few networks, of course, and nothing like Netflix or Amazon Prime or Hulu or any of those. So, it was really about the movies at that time.

So, yes, I did have an expectation, really not knowing how anything in the film industry worked. Of course, you get a lead in a film, and you're young, and you approach it with a fair amount of innocence. So, the expectation level is *huge*. Every movie is like, "Is this going to be something?" I don't think that feeling lasted as my career went on, because you learn the business and do what you do, and I think in those very, very early days, and in those early films of which *Thunder Alley* was one of, there definitely was *some* expectation, but what that expectation is defined at…a total unknown. The expectation is defined so much in a place and in an outcome, but more in *feeling*—"Oh, wouldn't it be wonderful if something wonderful from this happens?" That kind of thing.

Rhonda: I know what *Thunder Alley* means to me, but what does it mean to you, particularly then versus now?

Jill: I have always had a special love for this film. As my career went on…you know, you kind of forget about the job you did before or the job you did three jobs earlier and four jobs earlier, but then, as time goes on…. Then, in my case, where I left the business when I became pregnant with my eldest son, as time goes on—although I don't reflect upon any of the movies very often—but as time goes on and the movies come up, I would say that *Thunder Alley* is up there with a special love. I have a special love for the film. It's a small film. It's a tiny, tiny film. At the time I was making it, I didn't have a lot to compare it to, but now.... I fully understood it was a small movie; however, there was an intimacy to the entire filmmaking process on a small film like that. I don't think that quality is necessarily unique to just *Thunder Alley* in my career, but I think it's just a normal feeling—that feeling of intimacy—on small films. I just think it's normal. [*laughs*] The movie didn't really have any gratuitous nature to it, and I think that really helped cultivate the intimacy of the filmmaking process, both in front of the camera and behind the scenes. It was a family of people involved, and there was just unspoken intimacy that was present, I think, in making a film like that, which I love; it therefore has stayed with me over the years. Even though I don't think about it...if I think about it, it's there.

Rhonda: Did you think, while shooting, that the film's overall message is one that would still be so relevant and important over 30 years later?

Jill: I think you're probably talking about the...[*whispers*] drugs. [*laughs*] The lifestyle choices we make following our dreams, how we stay small, and how we choose to grow big and let ourselves blossom—I think the drugs aspect of the film is a wonderful parallel story to people given the choices in their lives, because I think we always say we're afraid of failure, but sometimes, I think we're more afraid of success. What if we become all of who we can be? What will our lives look like then? Will our friends still be our closest friends? Will my family look at me differently? Will I look at my family differently? Also, just the basic premise of be careful what you ask for, or be careful what you wish for, because it might come true...is it really, *really* what we want? Or is what we want just a picture of what we think we want? It's a great idea, but it's not really, really what we want. Or is it the hybrid version between those? I don't think we get to ever really know until, you know, you've done one thing or the other and things in between, and you look back in life and know much better, as we always do in retrospect...looking back in hindsight, which is always 20/20.

So, no; at the time, I never thought of it like that. But I think I resonated with the film, with the script. Some *thing* resonated in me right away, from day one, because of the basic humanity, and I think that's what the film really tapped into. It just showed basic humanity. In this case, it happened to be about that young man and his best friend and the set design, so to speak—the environment of that story was around music, and that was a beautiful environment, because music connects us all in so many ways. It really connects humanity. It doesn't matter what language it's sung in. We feel it, and that feeling communicates everything we really need to know about the song.

Rhonda: Do you have a favorite on-set memory?

Jill: Overall, I just really enjoyed making the film. Cynthia Eilbacher, who played my best friend in the film—she was just terrific. I was so in awe of her. She had this wonderful, big personality, and I was this quiet, shy girl. And then, we had all these *wonderful* young, talented actors and musicians on the set. Well, you know them; you saw the movie. [*laughs*] They were just a fantastic group of guys, and the director and his wife too—they were such lovely people. Everyone was fantastic. So, I don't know that I really have a favorite, but I do have an overall memory of it just being a really great experience. I would say a standout memory in terms of an "experience" would be when my character, Beth, falls into the water. There was frost on the ground, and it was the middle of the night, obviously, when we shot that, and I think it was near-freezing temperatures. It had to be in the 30s. It was really unbearable getting in that water. Although I had a wet suit on underneath my clothes, that first 2 to 3 minutes you are in there, it is freezing, freezing cold water and takes your breath away. It's one for the books. [*laughs*]

Rhonda: When you reflect on *Thunder* now, is there anything that stands out as specifically synchronistic or magical?

Jill: I love your question; I have to tell you that. I love those words, "synchronistic" and "magical." They happen to be two of my favorite words. I found out that *Alley*'s writer/director, Joe Cardone, went on and wrote the screenplay to *The Stepfather* (the remake), and I just found that very synchronistic, because what are the odds? [*laughs*] There are so many people in the world, so many people in entertainment, and here I starred in, oh, I don't know how many movies—15 movies, maybe—and one was *Thunder Alley* and one was *The Stepfather*, and Joe, whom I don't picture at all in my mind from having worked with him on *Thunder Alley*—I don't picture him being a *Stepfather* kind of screenwriter. But I say that not from a professional standpoint, but just the way I see him: There's nothing in the horror genre at all about him. I remember him being the loveliest guy, and he was very into music. It wouldn't surprise me at all if the film were semi-autobiographical about him; I don't know that for sure, although something rings true about that for me. I thought that was synchronistic. And then, about a year ago—I thought this was very odd: I was helping a friend of mine shoot a commercial, and they had this very young director on the set codirecting, and he's like, you know, "I think you know my mom's boyfriend." It was Scott McGinnis! Such a small world! I loved making that movie. I just loved it—and yeah…it was magical in that way for me.

Rhonda: Has there ever been talk of a reunion (of the cast, director, etc.) for a convention?

Jill: No, there never has been. It's a small movie, and not enough

Here's a nice one from The Stepfather, with Shelley Hack and Terry O'Quinn. © New Century Vista Film Company. (Jeez! I mean, All Rights Reserved.)

people saw the movie; however, people that have seen it have a special love for it. I don't know if this is true, what I heard, but about eight years ago, 10 years ago—somewhere in that time frame—I went into this store on Hollywood Boulevard, where I was told they had a lot of archival slides and stuff from films throughout the decades, and the man that owned the shop instantly knew me when I walked in. I said I was looking for photographs and slides from prior films I was in. He said, "I can't believe you've come into my store!" And I was like, "OK. Why? I'm nobody, but OK. Why?" [*laughs*] "It's so weird," he said. "Two nights ago, I was at this thing, and Quentin Tarantino was there speaking about his love of Cannon Films, and he mentioned *Thunder Alley* as one of his top three favorite—of all-time—Cannon Films." And that made me feel very special, to be a part of that in a kind of roundabout way. [*laughs*]

Rhonda: The music itself is such an important part of the film—its own character, really—and it looks like Roger Wilson and Leif Garrett are really singing (and the credits say as much). Was this something that was captured live—as in, were they really performing, or were they lip-synching and the music was added later? Were you on set much while the band/concert/rehearsal scenes were being shot? If so, I really want to know what you remember as standing out then and now.

Jill: Yes! Yes, it so is its own character! Roger and Leif *did* do their own singing. I think they prerecorded it, and then they performed back to what they recorded. That's how movies were done then, so I assume that's how it was. I was often on set when they did the musical numbers, though not all of them. I took advantage of when I wasn't in a scene to have a day off, but I was there at most of them. And Leif Garrett—I don't know what he's doing now. I know he's had his own struggles with addiction, but I can say he is a talented person. He had a beautiful voice; he was a very talented person.

Rhonda: Vinyl albums and soundtracks are hot once more. Is there anyone who owns the rights to the soundtrack that could potentially try to get it out there?

Jill: I *love* vinyl! I have no idea (about rights), but by far, the best person to ask would be Joe Cardone. And yes, people have periodically asked me about the soundtrack, but I get many more people asking for the soundtrack to a film I did called *Rich Girl* (1991). Then still, a lot of people have asked for the soundtrack to *The Phantom of the Opera* (1989), which was released, but not too many ask for *Thunder Alley*. But I have had a few ask, and that would be great, especially on vinyl. Anything can be produced and put out there in small quantities now for so little money. I have an original copy of *Thunder Alley*. Whenever I made a movie—of course, there was nothing digital at the time—I would get copies on three-quarter-inch tape back then, and very early on, I think I made digital copies as soon as we were able to make digital copies. So, I have quite a few that I made for myself. So, many people do ask, and I can't sell them, but I could give them to people who wanted them, and they could pay for shipping or something.

But I do have copies of the movie on DVD that I made some years back. I think the movie might have come out on laser disc. If it did, I have that as well. I think it would be great.

Rhonda: When you attend conventions, are you frequently asked about the soundtrack (and why there isn't one)?

Jill: This is heartbreaking, but not that many people ask me about *Thunder Alley*. The thing is, when they ask me about *Thunder Alley*, it is so special to them, and that makes it so special to me. I have a love for it, whereas I've grown to love a movie I did like *Popcorn* (1991), because it's meant so much to so many people… fans in the horror genre. But as a movie—and nothing against the horror fans of *Popcorn* because I love them all—my organic love would be for a *Thunder Alley* over *Popcorn*. It just has that special place in my heart.

Rhonda: I know you're a musician too. Do you have any upcoming releases or any projects I should let readers know about?

Jill: I do have some projects in production; I would feel better not talking about them until they are out and released 100 percent for sure, but I am busy at work. I can say one of them is a musical, but, you know, I really haven't been singing. I'll share…I don't know why, perhaps the COVID-19 thing, but I'll be more personal than I normally would be. I'll say that in June, it will be 12 years since I lost my partner. His name was Dave, and he was one of the world's greatest bass players. His name was Dave Carpenter. He played on so many soundtracks and at least 200 records. He was just a phenomenal stand-up bass player and played six-string bass guitar—he played it like a guitar. Anyway, we did so much music together. I met him doing my record, *Kelly's Smile*. When he died…I can't explain it. I guess I probably should have gone to therapy over it, but I didn't—I was too busy surviving—but when he died, I lost my love of music. Somehow, the music and his death…they were all tied together. I know one day I'll find it again—my love of music—in the way that I had it…in that beautiful, innocent, open, full-of-breath, life-affirming way. But his death was tough. I'll just say that. It was tough. He was young, and we'd been together for five and a half years when he died, and it just kind of took a piece of me when he left. That's all I'm gonna say about that, though I would love to…. It's so weird that I'm saying this now, because, earlier, I know I said that's all I'm going to say about that, but now I'm saying this…. It's very weird now…it's so weird that I'm thinking about—you used the word "synchronistic"—and I'm remembering that about three or four hours ago, I was talking to my mom, and she asked me what I was planning on doing with the rest of my day, and it's really odd, but I told her I feel like I need to sing. "I'm think I'm going to pull out music and sit down at the piano." I haven't played the piano in years and years and years, and I don't know why, but "I'm really feeling the need to connect," I told her, to the piano, to pull out my guitar. I really want to sing tonight. I'm having this spontaneous memory that only happened a few hours ago, and I am finding that incredibly synchronistic. And now I really will say that's all I'm going to say about that. I don't want to cry. [*laughs, but with a small catch in her voice*]

Rhonda: I'm seeing some bootlegging of *Thunder Alley* on DVD, but there's been no official release with all the extras it deserves! Do you know why?

Jill: I think it would be great if they had a release of it, but here's the thing with that: To do it right, it costs money, and I would imagine whoever owns the rights to it doesn't feel there'd be enough sales involved to warrant putting it out on DVD—however they do or redo these things. I don't know the real process; I just know there're lots of machines. I've done some interviews for other movies that they've put out for the first time on DVD, and that's the only reason I know even a tiny little bit about it, but what I do know about it, my knowledge is so microscopic that I'm embarrassed to even mention it. But I think it would be so great if they mentioned that—and they weren't bootlegged copies. Isn't that funny? I mentioned my bootleg copies. [*laughs*] My bootleg copies are good though. They're original. They really do come from the original three-quarter-inch that was sent to me within a month of the movie being finished. And I still have it, on three-quarter-inch.

THE RIAA'S LIST OF RECOMMENDATIONS

It is obviously not possible to define each individual situation in which a record label or artist should determine that a sound recording contains PAL Content. In making such a determination, however, record labels and artists should consider:

1. That contemporary cultural morals and standards should be used in determining whether parents or guardians would find the sound recording suitable for children;

2. The context in which the material is used, as some words, phrases, sounds, or descriptions might be offensive to parents if spotlighted or emphasized, but might not offend if merely part of the background or a minimal part of the lyrics;

3. The context of the artist performing the material, as well as the expectations of the artist's audience;

4. That lyrics are often susceptible to varying interpretations, and that words can have different meanings and should not be viewed in isolation from the music that accompanies them (i.e., lyrics when accompanied by loud and raucous music can be perceived differently than the same lyrics when accompanied by soft and soothing music);

5. That such a determination requires sensitivity and common sense, and that context, frequency, and emphasis are obviously important; isolated or unintelligible references to certain material might be insufficient to warrant labeling a particular sound recording as containing PAL Content;

6. That these Standards apply to the case of a single track commercially released as well as to full albums (whether released in the form of a CD, cassette or any other configuration); and

7. That a sound recording may contain strong language or depictions of violence, sex, or substance abuse, yet due to other factors involved, may not merit a designation as containing PAL Content.[1]

---

1 "PAL Standards." *Recording Industry Association of America*, www.riaa.com/resources-learning/pal-standards/

I'D BUY THAT FOR A DOLLAR!

BY MIKE HAUSHALTER

About the time I first started writing my column about dollar-movie-bin-diving for *Exploitation Nation*, I found out my wife and I would be soon moving into a new home. This was exciting news, and as I wrapped up my writing for the second issue of *EN*, I started packing up all of my movies, including a box full of dollar films I had purchased to use for future articles. Of course, when it came time to write my column for issues three and four, nearly all my films were still packed because, lo and behold, we had not moved yet, as things had gotten held up. So, I bought some new dollar movies to watch, wrote my reviews, and waited to move. When the time to write for the fifth issue came, I had finally moved and had even unpacked a good deal of my movie collection (not the forgotten box full of dollar titles, mind you, but I was OK because I, of course, had a second box full of films to watch and didn't really remember the first anymore). This continued until I finished my piece for the tenth issue, and as I searched for some other lost item that no longer matters at this point, I stumbled across my lost box and decided the time was nigh to dig through it and give some of the discs a review.

RAIDERS OF THE LOST BOX

Duel to the Death (1983)

The box says: The best swordsmen of China and Japan have made it a historical ritual to meet every 10 years for a showdown of fighting skills and powers. The leading fighter of the Japanese ninjas, Hashimoto (Tsui Siu Keung), and the Chinese chief Chin Wan (Damian Lau) have come to respect each other after years of competition—but tradition demands that they lock swords again. Their honor is put to the test when rogue ninjas barge into a Shaolin temple to steal a secret kung fu manuscript and unleash a war.

Directed by Tony Ching Siu-Tung (*Hero, City Hunter*), master of all the swashbuckling sword fights, *Duel to the Death* is the stuff that classic sword fight epics are made of. Besides a plot that keeps you tethered to the edge, *Duel to the Death* contains some of the most spectacular ninja-versus-swordsman action of all time, as well as some of the most gravity-defying wire stunts to be seen on screen.

Why I risked a dollar: This was not a risk as much as a must-have purchase, as I am a longtime fan of the film (ever since I was introduced to the title via John Saxon and *The Deadliest Art: The Best of the Martial Arts Films*). After losing my previous copy, I had wanted a new copy for my collection for some time.

Thoughts: As I began rifling through my lost box of dollar films to decide if it contained any review-worthy titles, I excitedly came across *Duel to the Death*. I initially put the film to the side to add to my "Hong Kong films" shelves. When I realized the lost box had plenty of content for an article, I decided since it had been so long since I had seen *Duel to the Death*, I would give the film a review to kick off my latest column. I am happy to say *Duel to the Death* lived up to my memories, and it was great to watch the film again. It's loaded with chivalry, swordplay, and kung fu action.

Plus: The film features a great story, wall-to-wall epic swordplay, a giant ninja, a flying ninja kite attack, exploding ninjas, a talking decapitated head, and a cliff-duel climax! *Duel to the Death* also has an awesome cast, including *Zu: Warriors from the Magic Mountain*'s Norman Chu (billed as Tsui Siu Keung) and Damian Lau, who share great chemistry as the film's two heroic swordsmen. Flora Chong-Leen (*The Head Hunter*) also appears as the beautiful but deadly swordswoman who wants to prove that she is as good as any man.

Minus: The film is overly grim, with perhaps a bit too much melodrama.

Shelf/Bin: It was on the shelf before I even finished writing all of this up. This is a fine example of '80s-era swordplay/wire work cinema, one that, unlike some of its cinematic cousins, does not get bogged down with silliness.

Lara Croft: Tomb Raider (2001)

The box says: Lara Croft, the world's most famous video game heroine, bursts onto the big screen in "...the most stylish and entertaining action-adventure movie in years!" Exploring lost empires, finding priceless treasures, punishing villains in mortal combat...it's all in a day's work for adventurer Lara Croft (Angelina Jolie). But a secret from her father's (Jon Voight) past is about to lead Lara to her greatest challenge: the Triangle of Light, a legendary artifact with the power to alter space and time. Lara must find the Triangle before it falls into the clutches of the Illuminati, a secret society bent on world domination. To stop the Illuminati, Lara will have to survive a cross-continental chase filled with unimaginable danger, but for the Tomb Raider, danger is the name of the game.

Why I risked a dollar: Back in the late '90s, I was a huge fan of the *Tomb Raider* games. I played them dang near nonstop on nights when my buddies were working and couldn't hang out for movie night. That said, I recall being pretty stoked for the release of the first *Tomb Raider* movie. I also recall being pretty let down by the film, so much so that I never watched it again, and I only watched its sequel after it had been on video for about a year. However, when I found the original (and the sequel) for a dollar more than a decade later, I figured it was time to give the film another shot (regardless of boxing it up and losing it for another three or so years).

Thoughts: It turns out that my memories of this one being a big letdown are pretty accurate, as that's how I would still best describe the film. It has a few moments of excitement here and there, as well as some decent special effects, but *Tomb Raider* is really nothing to write home about (or spend much effort talking about).

Plus: Angelina Jolie makes a fetching visual match for Lara Croft. There's also a bit of the famous *Tomb Raider* double-gun/gymnastic action, as well as a training robot, stone warrior automatons, and the Harryhausen-inspired boss beast. The film features Iain Glen as Manfred Powell, the film's James Bond-ish supervillain. Speaking of James Bond, future Bond Daniel Craig shows off his physique as the first Croft boy.

Minus: The film's storyline and dialogue don't live up to the video game source material. Jolie doesn't really seem to be sure of herself or her English accent. Staging, editing, and special effects sabotage what could have been some fantastic set pieces. Contributing to this overly underwhelming effort are the non-lethal gun fights, PG-13 rating, and lack of Lara Croft's trademark shorts.

Shelf/Bin: From one box to another: I am afraid to say this one is history.

Lara Croft Tomb Raider: The Cradle of Life (2003)

The box says: Lara Croft (Angelina

119

Jolie) is back in action and faces her most perilous mission: to recover what ancient civilization believed to be the essence of all evil, Pandora's Box. She must travel the globe, from Greece, to Hong Kong, to Kenya, and beyond to get to the box before it's found by a maniacal scientist whose plan is to use it for mass annihilation. For this adventure, Lara recruits her ex-partner—Terry Sheridan (Gerard Butler)—a dangerous mercenary who has previously betrayed Lara and their country. Join her as she races through furious hand-to-hand battles, blazing shoot-outs and breathtaking sky-diving escapes to try to save the ancient artifact...and mankind's future.

Why I risked a dollar: As previously stated, I was a pretty big fan of the game and was a bit disappointed in the films when they first came out. I picked up both films with high hopes that I would enjoy them both all these years later. I was wrong.

Thoughts: When I bought this, I had intended to double-feature it with the first *Tomb Raider* and revisit both films in one sitting. In fact, I was looking forward to it. But as the closing credits rolled on *Lara Croft: Tomb Raider*, I was far too disappointed and let down to even contemplate spending another two hours with the franchise. That said, a good two or so weeks later, I gave this film a watch and once again found myself underwhelmed by what could (and should) have been an exciting and fun outing. Of the two, this one may be slightly better, but neither has much to offer.

Plus: The sequel is a really good-looking film. There is lethal gunplay, a cliff-dive gun fight, pole-vaulting, and high-rise hang gliding. Gerard Butler is no Daniel Craig, but he gets to play a much better Croft boy.

Minus: Somehow, Angelina Jolie is worse here as Croft than in her first outing. She never looks as sexy as her video game namesake, but really, none of the film lives up to its video game namesake. Simon Yam's character is underwritten and underused. The monsters are also generic, and a shark gets punched.

Shelf/Bin: I put it right next to *Lara Croft: Tomb Raider* to wait out its trip to my favorite comic shop.

The Long Riders (1980)

The box says: Jesse James and his gang of outlaws ride again in this "extraordinary" (*Los Angeles Herald-Examiner*) Western that pulsates with hard-driving action and electrifying drama. Four sets of acclaimed actor brothers—Dennis and Randy Quaid; Stacy and James Keach; Christopher and Nicholas Guest; and Keith, Robert, and David Carradine—

each depict real-life siblings in emotionally charged portrayals of the Old West's legendary bandits. The notorious James-Younger gang is the most famous group of outlaws in the country, robbing banks, trains, and stagecoaches with a sense of daring that makes them folk heroes throughout the land. But when the mighty Pinkerton detective agency swears to track them down, these criminals must face an awesome enemy that will stop at nothing to see them behind bars...or dead! Only through the strength of their loyalty and blood ties can the outlaws hope to survive the brutal pursuits, unexpected betrayals, and blistering showdowns that mark the end of their dangerous ride.

Why I risked a dollar: I had been meaning to see this for decades but passed it up for one reason or another. At first, I was waiting for a chance to see it widescreen instead of pan-and-scanned. By the time a widescreen version became available, I had kind of forgotten about it. When I saw it on the shelf for a buck, I knew the time was right to finally give it a watch.

Thoughts: This is a top-drawer Western and may be one of Walter Hill's finest films. After having *The Long Riders* on my to-view list for decades, I was relieved that the film turned out to be a winner. I wouldn't say it is my favorite of Hill's films, as I enjoy both *Streets of Fire* and *Last Man Standing* more. Seeing it also made me realize I had missed a few other Hill films, such as *The Driver* and *Extreme Prejudice*. I discovered that *Extreme Prejudice* can only be watched as intended on a German import Blu-ray, so I requested *The Driver* from my local library and blind-bought the German import of *Extreme Prejudice* (a great film and wise purchase, it turns out).

Plus: The four real-life sets of brothers playing all the sibling characters is brilliant casting. The film features excellent ensemble storytelling, as well as great editing, brutal squibs, top-tier gunplay, and a knife-fight honor-duel. The soundtrack from Ry Cooder is also fantastic.

Minus: The film is episodic and slow-paced. At times, the horses are obviously put at risk.

Shelf/Bin: So, I really liked this one and recommend it to fans of Westerns and Walter Hill alike, but I am still probably going to bin this one. I enjoyed the film but find it unlikely that I will revisit it anytime in the next few years.

Screaming Dead (2003)

The box says: An abandoned insane asylum looms dark and foreboding on the horizon. Into it pass six individuals who are about to discover its terrifying secrets and come face to face with its blackest horrors.

Sleaze photographer Roger Neale and three beautiful models take up residence in a reportedly haunted old building—an ideal location for Neale's photographic "study in terror." The hospital was financed by a depraved industrialist who built a hidden vault under the basement where he tortured and murdered hundreds of patients. Neale himself is a sadist, and he takes great pleasure in exploiting the helpless young women. But when he discovers a secret passageway, it leads to a blood-splattered dungeon... and into a supernatural world where pain and evil await mortal flesh.

Why I risked a dollar: Years ago, when I wrote for *Secret Scroll Digest*, I frequently watched and reviewed E.I. Independent Cinema films. While I mostly enjoyed them, the E.I. films eventually began to blur together and lose their charm, so I dropped them from my viewing habits. Nowadays, E.I. films are mostly out of print and go for big bucks on eBay, so when I came across one for a dollar, it seemed like both an investment and a way to relive the old days. Then, it got packed away and forgotten, and perhaps rightfully, so it seems.

Thoughts: I watch a lot of exploitation films, as well as many things that are far from politically correct, without batting an eye, but this film just starts out kind of skeevy and only gets worse from there. While I think it was director Brett Piper's intent for the film to be "in your face" and push buttons, the degradation and mistreatment of the female characters feels a bit too real and more uncomfortable to watch than entertaining. Not only that, when the film switches gears to bring evil spirits into the mix, instead of revving up the menace, the film becomes rather mundane. To top it all off, I confused this film with one of Piper's others, *Shock-O-Rama*, so it wasn't even the movie I had wanted to see.

Plus: The cast is good, and the lead villain gets the beatdown he deserves by several characters and a ghost. There's brain goo! In addition, the conclusion is satisfying, with no annoying sting in the tail to snatch away the heroes' thunder; it's a *Pit and the Pendulum*-pastiche finale, complete with a fiery, Roger Corman-style end. While the film was pretty much a complete fail, the DVD had some cool bonus features, including a fun Misty Mundae featurette, a featurette on the asylum where the film was shot, and a *Fangoria* convention fluff piece.

Minus: Did I mention there isare some very uncomfortable character interactions and treatment of women? There are also bullies and bad special effects. The villain looks a lot like the director, which adds an extra level of ick. It's also just a drab-looking film.

Shelf/Bin I hit Play with a lot of hope and fond memories of this one. I realized very quickly, however, that I was out of luck, as this was not the film I thought it was, nor is it one I will be keeping.

Deep Impact (1998)

The box says: What would you do if you knew that in a handful of days, an enormous comet would collide with Earth and all humanity could be annihilated? The countdown to doomsday is underway in this "gut-wrenching, eye-opening blast of a movie experience" (Jeff Craig, *Sixty-Second Preview*). Mimi Leder (*The Peacemaker*) directs, guiding an all-star cast featuring Robert Duvall, Téa Leoni, Elijah Wood, Vanessa Redgrave, Maximilian Schell, and Morgan Freeman. With the film's dynamic fusion of large-scale excitement and touching, human-scale storylines, *Deep Impact* makes its impact felt in a big and unforgettable way.

Why I risked a dollar: I picked up *Deep Impact* because I am a big fan of disaster films and had never seen it. I also thought it would be a perfect example of the big-budget Hollywood film that I had overlooked not just when it first came out, but for the last 20-some years.

Thoughts: Back when *Deep Impact* came out, I chose to see its competitor, *Armageddon*, instead. Visually, *Armageddon* may have the edge, but in terms of sheer tension and story gravitas, *Deep Impact* is the clear winner. I am a bit disappointed in myself for not watching it sooner and for missing it in theaters.

Plus: It gives hope for humanity. The film has all the feels, as well as an outstanding cast that is a virtual Who's Who of future (and fading) stars. Morgan Freeman is amazing as the president of our country. The space heroics are also great.

Minus: It is a bit maudlin and perhaps a bit too real a threat for 2020 (At least there's no pandemic). The film drags a bit in parts, and there are too many characters. There is no fireman/police or other emergency responder presence, and animals being loaded up two by two is a bit too much. The sound design is also underwhelming.

Shelf/Bin: Despite liking this one a great deal, I'm still chucking it in the bin. Shelf space is precious, I won't likely watch this again for a long time, and it will be easy enough to get the film from the library or stream it the next time the urge to watch strikes me. From what I have read, the Blu-ray release wasn't that good, so it's not even worth an upgrade right now.

Back issue pages like REAL magazines used to have!
I mean, ALSO FROM HAPPY CLOUD MEDIA, LLC:

Exploitation Nation—Premiere Issue! We kick off with everyone's favorite sub-genre: the **Lesbian Vampire Film**. In this premiere issue, Dyanne Thorne interview; "lost" interviews with Clive Barker and his *Saint Sinner* stars, Mary Mara, Rebecca Harrell. Plus reviews! $5.99

#2: Cryptids of the Cinema: Bigfoot, Nessie, The Mothman, The Yeti, The Pope Lick Monster - we got 'em all! Well, most. The monsters and the movies that love them. Also this issue, journalist Mike Watt takes a look back at his time covering 2009's *Sorority Row*. Plus, bidding a fond farewell to **George A. Romero**. $7.99

#3: Bizarro Films. Contributions from Heather Drain and John Skipp. PLUS: Jose Mojica Marins, aka "Coffin Joe"; an interviews with filmmakers Rolfe Kanefsky; Greg DeLiso and Peter Litvin, and EXCLUSIVE INTERVIEW with Stephen Sayadian (aka "Rinse Dream"). $7.99

#4: Rock 'n Roll Movies! 144-pages! Interviews with Paul Bunnell (*The Ghastly Love of Johnny X*); Jon-Mikl Thor and Frank Dietz (*Rock 'n Roll Nightmare*); *Slade in Flame*; AIP's *Beach Party* films; Prince on Film; goodbye to Harlan Ellison; Richard Elfman on *Forbidden Zone*. $7.99

#5: Alternate Reality Warning: not a single title in this book is real. Interviewee Larry Blamire ("The Lost Skeleton Cadavra") is real, but the interview isn't. Plus: The Beatles' adapt *Lord Of The Rings*, directed by Stanley Kubrick; David Lynch directs *Revenge of the Jedi*; Amos Poe's remake of *Alphaville* with Debbie Harry; the film adaptation *A Field Guide To Film Gods*. ALL HAIL CINEMAGOG! $7.99

Order today at www.happycloudpublishing.com!

Back issue pages like REAL magazines used to have!
I mean, ALSO FROM HAPPY CLOUD MEDIA, LLC:

#6: Underground Comix! Did your old man throw YOURS away? Interviews with: Stephen Bissette, Trina Robbins, Mike Diana, Frank Henenlotter, Greg Ketter, Mark Bode, Howard Cruse's final interview; plus Buddy Giovinazzo, Vaughn Bode's final essay, *Confessions Of A Cartoon Gooroo*; Spaghetti Westerns, Robert Altman's *Popeye*, and a eulogy for Stan Lee.

Note: #6 Boasts two covers, sold separately:

COVER A - Mark Bode's mural from San Francisco's Clarion Alley.

COVER B - Will Eisner's art for Denis Kitchen's SNARF #3.

$7.99 each

#7: Indie Filmmaking issue! * Mark Savage and his new film *Purgatory Road*; James L. Edwards and *Her Name Was Christa** Gabe Bartalos and his newest, *Saint Bernard** Scooter McCrae and his adventures with the British censorship; Carmine Capobianco (*Psychos in Love*); Henrique Couto (*Babysitter Massacre*); Revjen Miller (*The Adventures of Electra Elf*). $7.99

#8: Witnesses for the Defense! Our writers to defend a movie only they seem to like. From *Grease 2* to *Ernest Goes to Jail* to *Godzilla '98*. PLUS an **exclusive interview with director Terry Gilliam** and *The Man Who Killed Don Quixote*! $7.99

#9: When Nature (and Elder Gods) Attack! Cover by interviewee Tom Sullivan (*Evil Dead*)! PLUS a tribute to Stuart Gordon; Lovecraft movies; Tippi Hedren tries to kill her family in *Roar!*, Asian Worm Horror! And much more! $7.99

Order today at www.happycloudpublishing.com!

Back issue pages like REAL magazines used to have!
I mean, ALSO FROM HAPPY CLOUD MEDIA, LLC:

Grindhouse Purgatory #12 is a special ALL SOMETHING WEIRD VIDEO Issue paying tribute to that all-important label we know and cherish. Contents include memories of SWV founder Mike Vraney; tributes to Herschell Gordon Lewis, David F. Friedman; a word from Frank Henenlotter; a look at those Sexy Shockers, Drivers-Ed, and Health Scare films, and much, much more! $9.99

GP #15: In this special issue, we say goodbye to our friend, actor, and mentor, Sid Haig. His friends and fans come from all over contribute remembrances of this amazing man and his incredible career. From his early days starring in Jack Hill's exploitation epics, to his resurgence in *Jackie Brown* and *House of 1,000 Corpses*, Sid was a unique performer and a lovely person. $9.99

Grindhouse Purgatory Greatest Hits: collecting the best material from the now out-of-print Issues 1-3, along with some brand new material unavailable anywhere else. Spaghetti Westerns! Hardcore Wrestling! *Codename: Wild Geese*! The forgotten beauty of '70s 42nd Street! Plus a little tribute to our departed friend, Andy Copp. And much more! $9.99

Order today at www.happycloudpublishing.com!

Back issue pages like REAL magazines used to have!
I mean, ALSO FROM HAPPY CLOUD MEDIA, LLC:

Hot Splices by Mike Watt. Eight interwoven tales about the Film Addicts, the Cinephages who devour film for the high, the bleeding perforations in their skin is just part of the game. There are five forbidden films that can induce madness or release the Dark Gods that created them, speaking through the psychopathic director. Fiction. $14.99

Night of the Living Dead '90: The Version You've Never Seen by Tom Savini. Take a look at the intended version of Tom Savini's remake of *Night of the Living Dead 1990*, thorugh this unique book collecting the full storyboards for this film for the first time. Thirty years after the fact, the true story can be told. With annotations by the director and exclusive photographs! This is a unique look at a classic film. $29.99

Shadows & Light: Journeys With Outlaws in Revolutionary Hollywood by Gary Kent. Writer, director, actor, stuntman, special effects guru, production manager Gary Kent tells his Hollywood story, chronicling his adventures with Brian De Palma, Bruce Campbell, Ed Wood, Charles Manson, Frank Zappa, the Hells Angels and others. This is the first printing from Happy Cloud Media, LLC, with an updated Afterword. $19.99

A Whole Bag of Crazy: Sordid Tales of Hookers, Weed, and Grindhouse Movies by Pete Chiarella. Hustler, pot fiend, porn expert.Take a walk down a dark alley with 42nd Street Pete as he recounts his tales growing up on "The Deuce". Criminal activity, classic undesirable cinema, pot, booze, pros, cons. The '70s: uncut, uncensored. If you really remember the '70s, you were lucky to have survived them. $14.99

Order today at www.happycloudpublishing.com!

Back issue pages like REAL magazines used to have!
I mean, ALSO FROM HAPPY CLOUD MEDIA, LLC:

Movie Outlaw: The Prequel by Mike Watt is a revamped republishing of what was previously-known as *Fervid Filmmaking*. Featuring essays on 70 underseen films including *Keep Off My Grass*, *Dr. Caligari*, *Forbidden Zone*, *Coonskin*, *Head*, *Psychos in Love*, and many more. A rare interview with director Stephen Sayadian. 350 pages. $15.99

Movie Outlaw by Mike Watt. Essays focusing on more than 70 underseen films including Johnny Depp's directorial debut, *The Brave*; *Don's Plum*; Mauritzio Nichetti's *Volere Volare*; *The Ghastly Love of Johnny X*, the last 35mm black 'n white science fictional musical ever made! 472 pages. $19.99

Movie Outlaw Rides Again! By Mike Watt. Essays on 70 underseen films: *Crazy Moon*; *Frankenhooker*; *Jane White is Sick and Twisted*; *The Magic Christian*, *Meet the Feebles*; *Impure Thoughts*; *The Stunt Man*; *Night Breed*; Brian DePalma's *Phantom of the Paradise*, Will Vinton's *The Adventures of Mark Twain*; *The Redsin Tower*. 392 pages. $19.99

Son of the Return of Movie Outlaw by Mike Watt. Essays include: *Accion Mutante;* Ralph Bakshi's *Heavy Traffic*; *Down and Dirty Duck*; *The Thief and the Cobbler*; *The Sinful Dwarf*; *Performance*; *Muppets Most Wanted*; *Legend of Simon Conjurer*; *Sorority Babes in the Slimeball Bowl-O-Rama*; *Shock Treatment*; *Yellowbeard*. Interviews with Jon Voight and Ralph Bakshi! 352 pages. $19.99

Order today at www.happycloudpublishing.com!

www.ingramcontent.com/pod-product-compliance
Lightning Source LLC
Chambersburg PA
CBHW071517040426
42444CB00008B/1692